Buenos Aires Travel Guide 2026

Discover Culture, Cuisine, Tango, and Hidden Experiences in Arg   al

Julian R. Jeremy

COPYRIGHT

All rights reserved © 2025

No part of this publication may be reproduced, distributed, stored in a retrieval system, or transmitted in any form or by any means—electronic, mechanical, photocopying, recording, or otherwise—without the prior written permission of the author, except for brief quotations used in reviews or scholarly works.

TABLE OF CONTENTS

COPYRIGHT	**2**
TABLE OF CONTENTS	**3**
INTRODUCTION	**6**
Why Visit Buenos Aires in 2026	6
Quick Facts & Snapshot	7
How to Use This Guide	8
CHAPTER 1: A BRIEF HISTORY & CULTURE OF BUENOS AIRES	**14**
Colonial Past & European Influence	14
Tango: More Than a Dance	15
Porteño Lifestyle & Local Traditions	16
Festivals & Annual Events in 2026	17
CHAPTER 2: TOP ATTRACTIONS & DESTINATIONS	**19**
Plaza de Mayo & Casa Rosada	19
Recoleta Cemetery	22
Teatro Colón	26
La Boca & Caminito Street	30
San Telmo	34
Puerto Madero	38
Palermo	43
Museo Nacional de Bellas Artes	47
Obelisco & Avenida 9 de Julio	50
Day Trip Highlights Nearby	54
CHAPTER 3: GETTING THERE & GETTING AROUND	**58**
Visa & Entry Requirements for 2026	60
Public Transportation	61
Navigating the City on Foot & Bike	62
Safety Tips for Transport	64
CHAPTER 4: ACCOMMODATION IN BUENOS AIRES	**66**

Budget Stays	66
Mid-Range Options	68
Luxury Hotels	71
Best Neighborhoods to Stay	73

CHAPTER 5: FOOD & NIGHTLIFE — 75

Traditional Argentine Cuisine	75
Must-Try Street Foods	77
Cafés & Historic Coffee Houses	79
Fine Dining & Michelin-Listed Restaurants	81
Wine & Malbec Culture	83
Nightlife: Tango Shows, Clubs & Bars	84

CHAPTER 6: SHOPPING & LOCAL MARKETS — 87

Souvenirs Worth Bringing Home	87
Feria de San Telmo (Antique Market)	88
Palermo Soho & Palermo Hollywood Boutiques	89
Leather Goods, Crafts, and Art	90
Shopping Malls & Modern Retail	91

CHAPTER 7: ITINERARIES — 94

3-Day Itinerary	94
5-Day Itinerary	95
7-Day Itinerary	96

CHAPTER 8: HIDDEN GEMS OF BUENOS AIRES — 98

Neighborhoods Off the Beaten Path	98
Secret Rooftop Bars & Cafés	101
Little-Known Museums & Street Art Spots	104
Hidden Tango Milongas	106
Quiet Parks & Local Hangouts	108

CHAPTER 9: LANGUAGE, ETIQUETTE & COMMUNICATION — 111

Essential Spanish Phrases for Travelers	111
Polite Customs & Social Etiquette	112
How to Interact with Locals	112
Using English vs. Spanish in 2026	113

SIM Cards, Internet & Staying Connected 114
CHAPTER 10: PRACTICAL TIPS FOR TRAVELERS **116**
Currency & Money Matters 116
Safety & Common Scams 117
Health, Emergency Numbers & Pharmacies 118
Packing List Essentials for Buenos Aires 118
Seasonal Weather Guide 119
CONCLUSION **121**
Why Buenos Aires Will Leave You Wanting More 121
Inspiring Final Thoughts 121

INTRODUCTION

Why Visit Buenos Aires in 2026

Buenos Aires has long been one of South America's most captivating capitals, but 2026 is a particularly exciting time to visit. The city is undergoing a wave of cultural renewal, with new art spaces opening, revitalized historic neighborhoods, and major international events drawing visitors from around the globe. Argentina's renowned hospitality and the warmth of the porteños—the people of Buenos Aires—make it a destination that combines old-world European elegance with Latin American energy.

In 2026, Buenos Aires continues to be a cultural powerhouse, famous for its tango, world-class steak and Malbec wine, vibrant nightlife, and eclectic architecture. The city has also become a hotspot for digital nomads and long-term travelers, thanks to improved internet connectivity and government initiatives to welcome remote workers. With its mix of historic charm and modern flair, Buenos Aires offers something for every kind of traveler—whether you're a history buff, a foodie, a nightlife seeker, or simply someone who wants to experience a city that never seems to sleep.

Quick Facts & Snapshot

Location: Capital of Argentina, situated along the Río de la Plata on the southeastern coast of South America.

Population: Over 15 million in the greater metropolitan area, making it one of the largest cities in the Americas.

Language: Spanish is the official language, but English is widely spoken in tourist areas. Learning a few basic Spanish phrases will enrich your experience.

Currency: Argentine Peso (ARS). Exchange rates can be volatile, so travelers should stay updated and consider using cards or USD cash for stability.

Time Zone: Argentina Standard Time (GMT -3).

Climate: Temperate. Summers (December to February) are hot and humid, winters (June to August) are mild, and spring/autumn are pleasant for exploring.

Best Time to Visit: March–May and September–November, when temperatures are comfortable and cultural events fill the calendar.

Famous For: Tango music and dance, rich culinary traditions, historic neighborhoods, world-class art museums, lively markets, and passionate football culture.

How to Use This Guide

This guide is designed to be practical, easy to navigate, and packed with updated information for 2026. Each chapter has been organized so that you can dip into the sections most relevant to your style of travel.

If you want to explore the most famous attractions, go straight to the chapter on Top Attractions & Destinations.

If your priority is comfort and lodging, the dedicated Accommodation chapter outlines the best budget, mid-range, and luxury stays.

For travelers looking to plan their days, the Itineraries section offers ready-made suggestions for 3, 5, and 7 days in the city.

Adventurous travelers should not miss the Hidden Gems chapter, where we spotlight lesser-known neighborhoods, cafés, and experiences.

For those who like to plan every detail, the chapters on Food, Shopping, Getting Around, and Practical Tips will provide all the insider knowledge you need.

Throughout the guide, costs, transport options, opening hours, and local advice are clearly outlined to make planning easy. Whether you are visiting Buenos Aires for a quick city break, an extended stay, or as part of a larger South American adventure, this guide will help you experience the very best of the city in 2026.

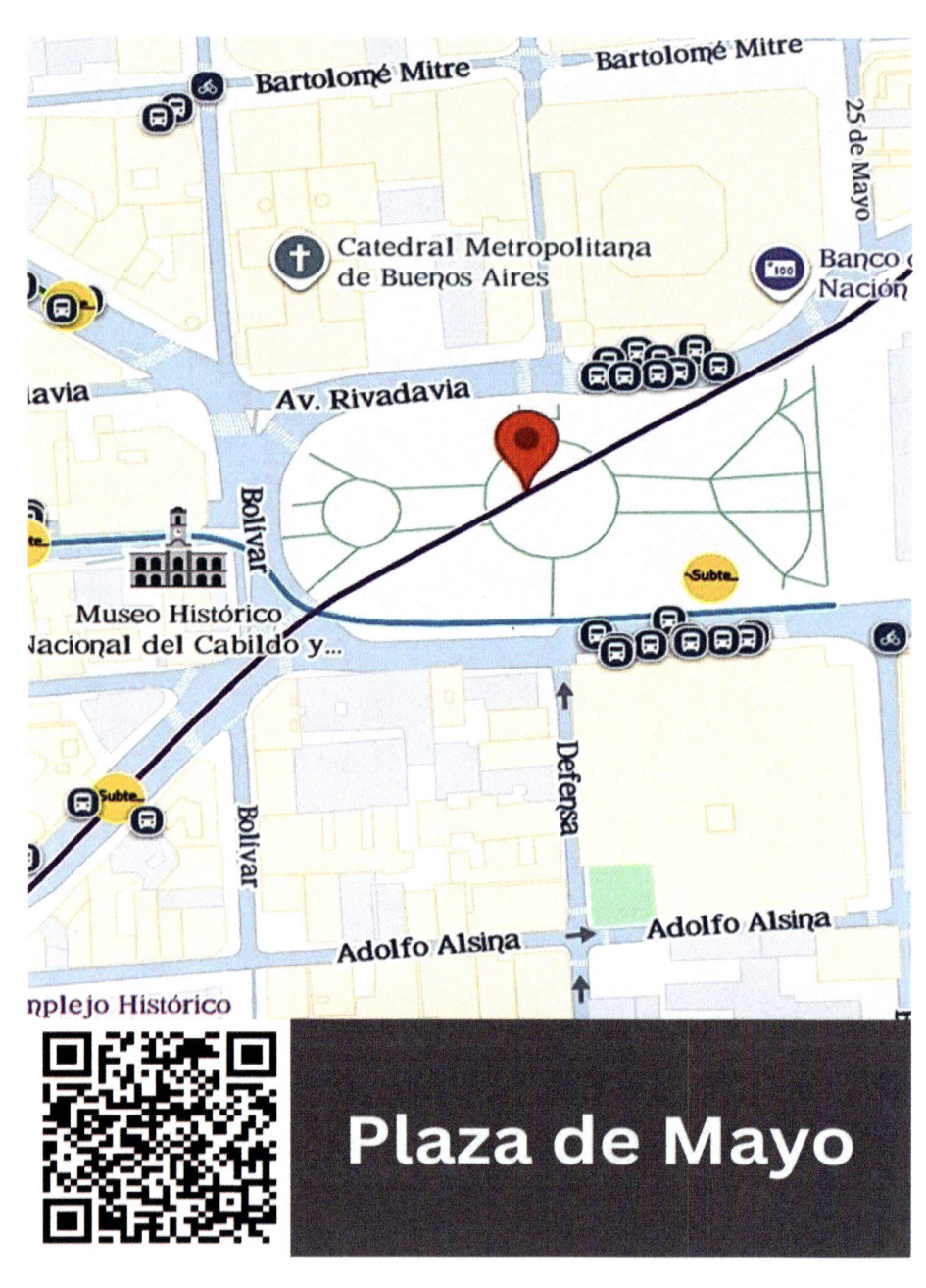

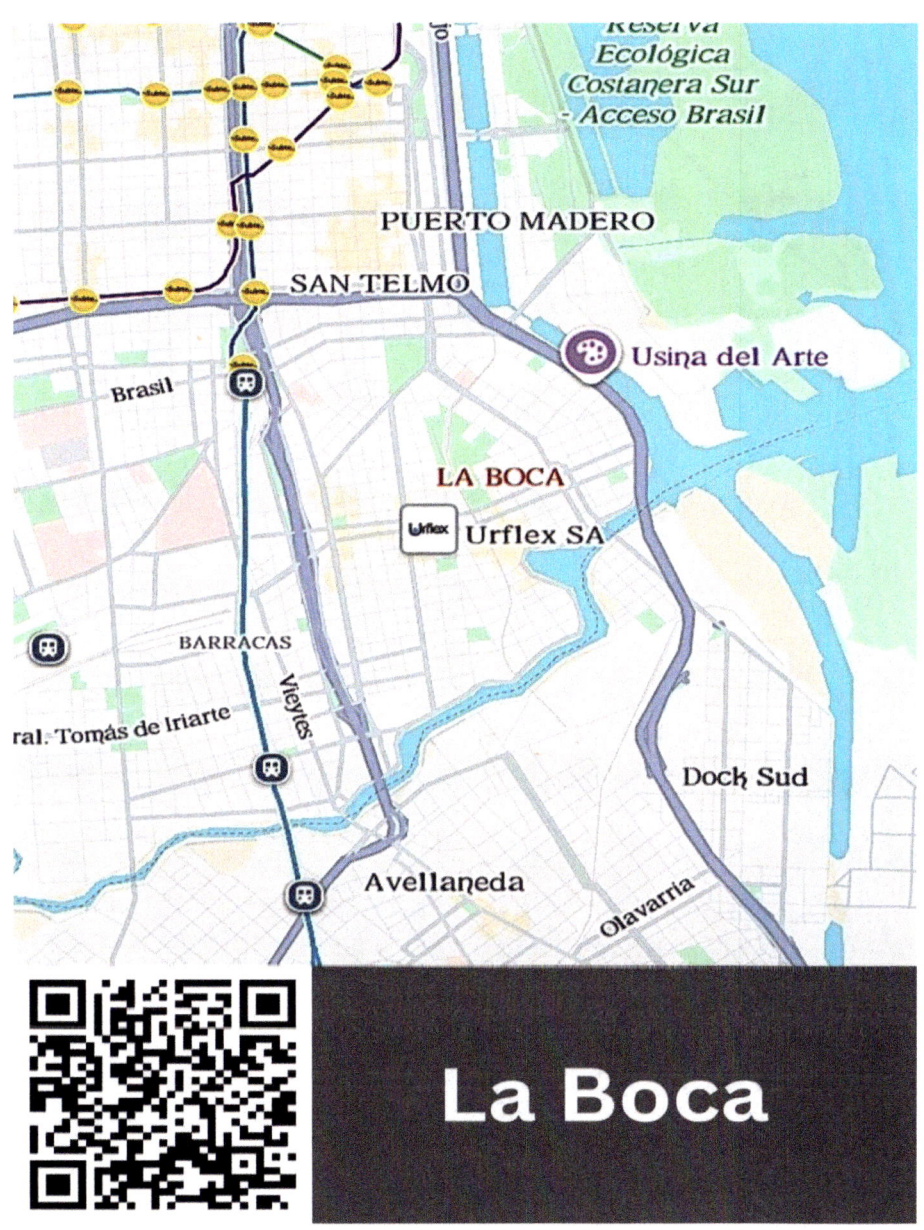

La Boca

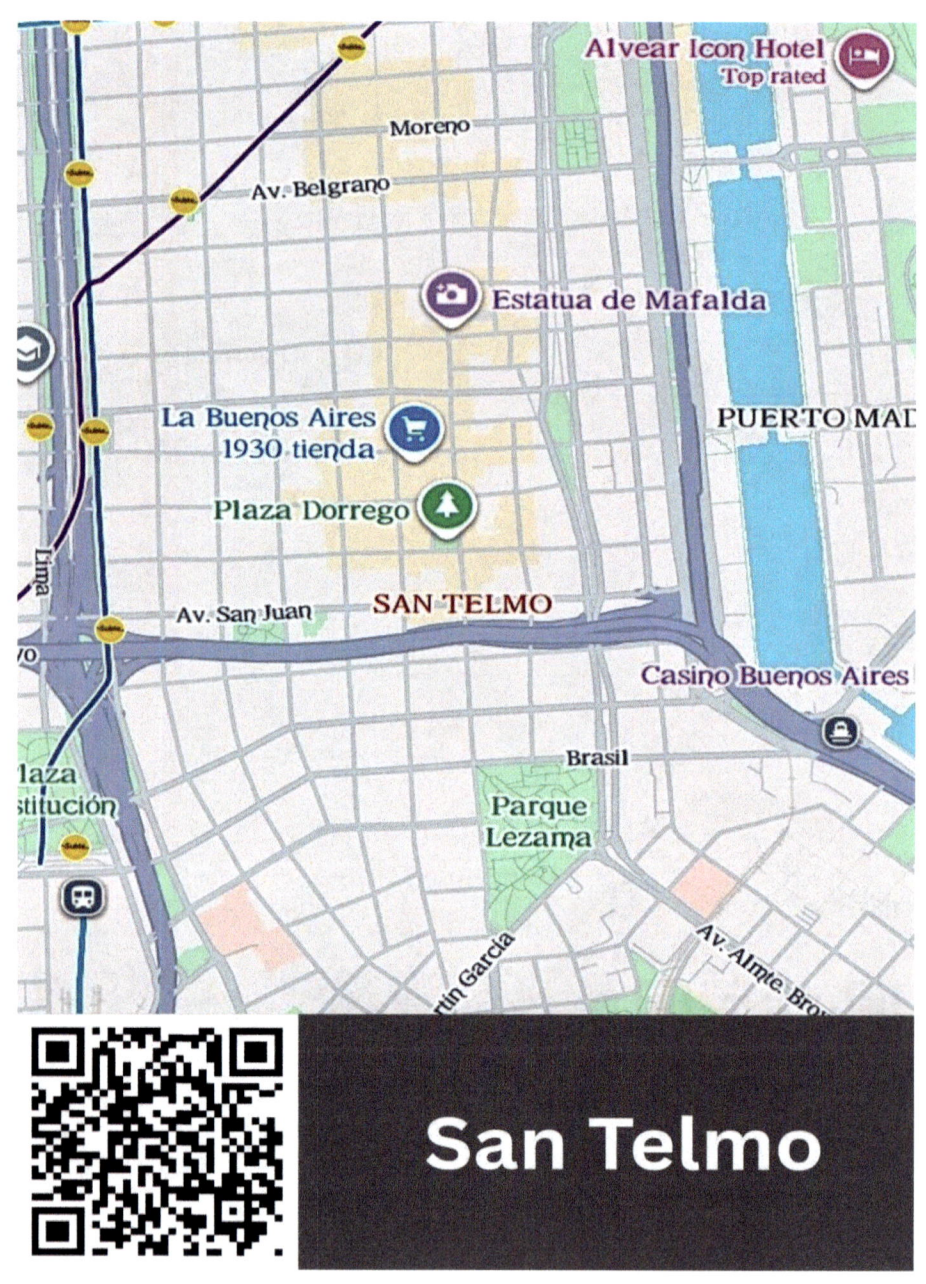

Puerto Madero

CHAPTER 1: A BRIEF HISTORY & CULTURE OF BUENOS AIRES

Colonial Past & European Influence

Buenos Aires traces its origins back to the early 16th century, when Spanish explorers first landed along the Río de la Plata. Although the initial settlements struggled, by 1580 the city was firmly re-established under Juan de Garay. Over the centuries, Buenos Aires became a thriving port city, acting as a vital link between Europe and South America.

Its architecture and urban planning still reflect these European roots. Walking through the streets, travelers notice neoclassical façades, French-style mansions, and Italianate courtyards. This blend of Spanish colonial foundations with later French and Italian influences gave Buenos Aires its reputation as the "Paris of South America." Wealth from cattle, leather, and grain exports in the 19th and early 20th centuries funded the construction of grand avenues and opera houses, most famously the Teatro Colón.

Yet, beneath this European veneer lies a uniquely Argentine identity. Waves of immigrants—from Italy, Spain, Germany, and Eastern Europe—shaped the city into a multicultural hub. They brought their foods, customs, and languages, creating the diverse melting pot that modern visitors still experience in its cafés, restaurants, and neighborhoods.

Tango: More Than a Dance

Tango is often described as the heartbeat of Buenos Aires. Born in the working-class neighborhoods of La Boca and San Telmo in the late 19th century, tango emerged from the meeting of cultures: African rhythms, European instruments, and local criollo traditions. What began as an expression of longing and melancholy among immigrants soon transformed into Argentina's most iconic cultural export.

Today, tango is more than just music and dance—it's a way of life. Milongas (social dance halls) continue to thrive across the city, where locals and visitors gather to dance until the early hours of the morning. Tango shows, ranging from intimate performances to large theatrical productions, allow travelers to experience its evolution from street corners to glamorous stages. UNESCO even declared tango part of the world's Intangible Cultural Heritage, underlining its cultural significance.

For travelers in 2026, the tango scene has grown even more accessible, with workshops and lessons tailored for beginners. Whether watching a polished show in a theater or slipping into a neighborhood milonga, engaging with tango offers an authentic window into Buenos Aires' soul.

Porteño Lifestyle & Local Traditions

The people of Buenos Aires proudly call themselves porteños, meaning "people of the port." This identity is shaped by their history as traders and immigrants, and it reflects in their openness, expressiveness, and pride in their city. Porteños are known for their passion—whether for politics, football, or long debates over coffee in historic cafés.

One of the most recognizable traditions is the culture of sharing mate, a strong herbal infusion sipped through a metal straw (bombilla) from a shared gourd. More than just a drink, mate represents community, hospitality, and conversation. Don't be surprised if locals offer visitors a sip—it's a gesture of inclusion.

Food also plays a central role in daily life. From leisurely Sunday asados (barbecues) with family to quick stops at neighborhood bakeries for medialunas (croissants), food is both ritual and social glue. Dinner is often eaten late, sometimes starting after 9 p.m., reflecting the city's night-owl rhythm.

The city's passion for football is another cultural pillar. Clubs like Boca Juniors and River Plate dominate conversations and shape identities. Attending a match at La Bombonera stadium or watching a local game in a neighborhood bar provides a powerful insight into this fiery tradition.

Festivals & Annual Events in 2026

Buenos Aires is a city that thrives on festivals and cultural events, and 2026 promises a vibrant calendar. These celebrations bring together locals and visitors, offering opportunities to experience Argentine traditions firsthand.

Buenos Aires Tango Festival and World Cup (August): The largest tango event in the world, featuring free classes, concerts, and competitions where dancers from across the globe compete for the title of world champions.

Carnival (February): Though smaller than Brazil's, Buenos Aires' carnival is lively, especially in neighborhoods like Boedo and San Telmo. Expect colorful parades, drumlines (murgas), and street dancing.

International Book Fair (April–May): One of the most important literary events in Latin America, attracting authors, publishers, and readers from around the world. Perfect for travelers interested in Argentine and global literature.

Buenos Aires International Festival of Independent Cinema (April): A celebration of cutting-edge cinema, screening films from local and international directors.

Noche de los Museos (Night of the Museums, November): Museums and cultural centers across the city open their doors late into the night with free admission, performances, and guided tours.

Food & Wine Festivals (throughout the year): Events like Caminos y Sabores highlight Argentine gastronomy, wine culture, and regional delicacies, allowing visitors to taste the country's diversity without leaving the city.

In 2026, Buenos Aires is also expected to host a series of cultural showcases tied to Argentina's preparations for future international sporting and cultural exchanges, further energizing the local arts and performance scene.

This expanded chapter sets the cultural tone for the guide—mixing history, traditions, and 2026 updates—while keeping it engaging for travelers.

CHAPTER 2: TOP ATTRACTIONS & DESTINATIONS

Plaza de Mayo & Casa Rosada

Plaza de Mayo: The Heart of Buenos Aires
Plaza de Mayo is the historic and political epicenter of Buenos Aires. Surrounded by some of the city's most important buildings, the square has been the stage for major national events since Argentina's independence in 1810. The square itself is named after the May Revolution, which began here and paved the way for Argentina's independence from Spain.

The plaza is not only beautiful, with fountains, statues, and manicured greenery, but also deeply symbolic. It has hosted presidential speeches, protests, and public celebrations. Travelers visiting in 2026 will still find it a gathering place for demonstrations, the most famous being the weekly march of the Mothers of Plaza de Mayo, who continue to demand justice for children who disappeared during Argentina's military dictatorship (1976–1983).

Key highlights inside Plaza de Mayo include:
- **Pyramid of May (Pirámide de Mayo)** – the oldest national monument in Buenos Aires, built in 1811.

- **Equestrian statue of General Manuel Belgrano** – creator of the Argentine flag.

- **Mothers of Plaza de Mayo march** – held every Thursday afternoon, a powerful and emotional sight for visitors.

Practical Information:
Location: Plaza de Mayo, Av. Hipólito Yrigoyen 219, C1089ABA, Buenos Aires.
Opening Hours: The square itself is open 24/7 as it is a public space.
Cost of Access: Free.
How to Get There: The easiest way is via the Subte (metro). Take Line A, D, or E to Estación Catedral, which exits directly at Plaza de Mayo. Bus lines 28, 56, 59, and 64 also stop nearby. For those walking from Microcentro, it's just a short walk down Avenida de Mayo.

Casa Rosada: The Pink Presidential Palace
At the eastern end of Plaza de Mayo stands the iconic Casa Rosada, Argentina's presidential palace and one of Buenos Aires' most recognizable landmarks. Its pink façade has sparked endless theories: some say it was painted to symbolize unity between political factions (red for Federalists and white for Unitarians), while others believe the pink came from mixing cow's blood with white paint in the 19th century.

Casa Rosada is not just an office building—it is a living symbol of Argentina's politics. From its famous balcony, leaders such as Eva Perón and Juan Domingo Perón addressed massive crowds gathered in

Plaza de Mayo, moments immortalized in Argentine history and popular culture (most notably in the musical Evita).

Inside, visitors can explore elegant salons, historic chambers, and even the presidential office. A highlight is the Casa Rosada Museum, located beneath the palace, which displays artifacts, documents, and personal belongings of past presidents.

Practical Information:
Location: Casa Rosada, Balcarce 50, C1064AAB, Buenos Aires.
Opening Hours: Guided tours are available on Saturdays, Sundays, and public holidays from 10:00 a.m. to 6:00 p.m. (last entry at 5:30 p.m.). Museum hours are typically Wednesday to Sunday from 10:00 a.m. to 6:00 p.m.
Cost of Access: Entrance is free, but advance online registration is recommended for guided tours due to limited spots.
How to Get There: Same as Plaza de Mayo—Subte Line A, D, or E to Catedral or Plaza de Mayo station. Visitors can also take a taxi or

rideshare to Balcarce 50. It is within walking distance from most downtown hotels.

Tips: Bring a valid ID (passport recommended) for security checks. Photography is allowed in most areas, but flash may be restricted. Weekends tend to be crowded, so visiting early in the day is advised.

Traveler Insights
For travelers in 2026, combining a visit to Plaza de Mayo with Casa Rosada is an unmissable introduction to Argentine history and politics. Spend some time sitting on a bench in the plaza, watching locals go about their routines, then step inside Casa Rosada for a glimpse into the nation's political heart.

Nearby cafés such as London City Café (Av. de Mayo 599) or the traditional Café Tortoni (a short walk on Av. de Mayo 825) make excellent stops for a coffee or snack after exploring. Pairing this visit with a walk down Avenida de Mayo, which connects Plaza de Mayo to the National Congress, creates a full half-day itinerary filled with history, architecture, and local flavor.

Recoleta Cemetery

A City of the Dead with Stories of the Living
Recoleta Cemetery (Cementerio de la Recoleta) is not just a burial ground—it is one of Buenos Aires' most extraordinary landmarks, blending history, art, and legend. Opened in 1822, it was the city's first public cemetery and quickly became the final resting place of Argentina's elite: presidents, generals, Nobel Prize winners, and cultural icons.

Walking through Recoleta Cemetery feels like exploring an open-air museum. Narrow cobbled walkways wind between ornate mausoleums built in Gothic, Art Deco, Baroque, and Art Nouveau styles. Many of these family vaults are topped with angels, crosses, and statues carved by Italian and French artists, making it a destination for art lovers as much as for history enthusiasts.

Today, Recoleta is ranked among the most beautiful cemeteries in the world, often compared with Père Lachaise in Paris. It attracts both locals and travelers eager to discover Argentina's history through the lives—and deaths—of its most notable figures.

The Tomb of Eva Perón (Evita)
The most visited tomb in Recoleta belongs to María Eva Duarte de Perón (Evita), Argentina's beloved First Lady from 1946 to 1952. Though her tomb is relatively modest compared to some of the grand mausoleums, it is always surrounded by flowers, handwritten notes, and tributes from admirers.

Eva Perón's journey to her final resting place was long and complicated: after her death in 1952, her body was hidden for nearly two decades before being returned to Argentina. Her presence in Recoleta adds to the cemetery's mystique, drawing thousands of visitors each year who wish to pay respects to a woman who remains a symbol of social justice and compassion for Argentina's working class.

Other Notable Residents

Beyond Evita, visitors will find tombs of many influential figures:

- **Domingo Faustino Sarmiento** – former president and educator, honored with a mausoleum topped by a condor.

- **Raúl Alfonsín** – the first democratically elected president after Argentina's dictatorship in 1983.

- **Luis Ángel Firpo** – the legendary boxer known as "The Wild Bull of the Pampas."

- **Admiral Guillermo Brown** – founder of the Argentine navy.

Each tomb tells a story, some tragic, some inspiring, giving visitors a sense of Argentina's turbulent but rich history.

Practical Information

Location: Junín 1760, C1113 CABA, Buenos Aires, Argentina.
Opening Hours: Open daily from 7:00 a.m. to 5:00 p.m. (last entry at 4:45 p.m.).
Cost of Access: General entry is free as of 2026, though guided tours (offered in English and Spanish) usually cost around ARS 3,000–5,000 (approx. USD $4–6). Some premium private tours can cost up to ARS 15,000 (USD $18) depending on group size and inclusions.
How to Get There:
Subte (Metro): Take Line H to Las Heras Station, a 5-minute walk from the cemetery entrance.
Bus: Several bus lines stop nearby, including lines 17, 61, and 67.
Taxi/Rideshare: A convenient option if coming from central Buenos Aires (10–15 minutes from Microcentro).
Facilities: Restrooms are available near the entrance. There are also cafés and restaurants around the cemetery's perimeter, perfect for a break after your visit.

Traveler Insights & Tips
- **Maps Are Essential** – The cemetery can feel like a maze, with over 6,000 mausoleums spread across its grounds. Maps are available at the entrance, or you can download digital maps in advance to locate Evita's tomb and other notable figures.

- **Best Time to Visit** – Arrive early in the morning for a quieter, more atmospheric experience. Afternoons tend to be busier, especially on weekends.

- **Guided Tours** – Joining a guided tour can enrich the experience with stories about the families, scandals, and mysteries behind the tombs. English tours often run in the mornings.

- **Photography** – Photography is allowed, and the play of light and shadow among the mausoleums makes for dramatic photos. Respect quiet areas where locals are visiting relatives' tombs.

- **Nearby Attractions** – After visiting, explore the Recoleta neighborhood, known for its cultural institutions like the Museo Nacional de Bellas Artes, the Floralis Genérica (a giant steel flower sculpture), and upscale cafés. The Recoleta Cultural Center and weekend Recoleta Handicraft Fair are right next to the cemetery and worth adding to your itinerary.

A Visit Worth More Than Curiosity
While some may hesitate at the thought of visiting a cemetery, Recoleta is one of the most enlightening experiences Buenos Aires has to offer. It provides a unique perspective on the city's history, its social classes, and its obsession with legacy. Standing in front of Evita's tomb or gazing up at the marble angels, travelers will understand why this cemetery is not just a place of rest—it's a mirror of Argentina itself.

Teatro Colón

A Stage That Defines Buenos Aires
The Teatro Colón is not only Argentina's most prestigious opera house but also one of the finest performance venues in the world. Since its inauguration in 1908, it has been celebrated for its exceptional acoustics, opulent architecture, and cultural significance. For over a century, it has hosted world-renowned artists such as Luciano Pavarotti, Maria Callas, Plácido Domingo, and ballet icons like Rudolf Nureyev.

Designed by a mix of Italian, French, and Argentine architects, Teatro Colón combines neoclassical and eclectic styles. Its grand façade, intricate interior details, and the massive chandelier hanging above the main hall reflect Buenos Aires' ambition during its golden age, when the city rivaled the great capitals of Europe.

The Opera House Experience

The main hall of Teatro Colón seats almost 2,500 guests and is ranked among the top five concert venues worldwide for acoustic quality. The U-shaped design, wooden floors, and carefully engineered dome create sound so pure that performers often say microphones are unnecessary.

Beyond opera, the theater hosts ballet, symphony concerts, and international music festivals. Its resident companies, including the Buenos Aires Philharmonic Orchestra and Ballet Estable del Teatro Colón, ensure a packed calendar throughout the year. For travelers in 2026, attending a live performance is considered a must-do cultural experience in Buenos Aires.

Guided Tours

For those who cannot attend a show, guided tours provide access to the theater's most stunning spaces:

- The Main Foyer, adorned with marble columns and Venetian mosaics.

- The Golden Hall (Salón Dorado), decorated with chandeliers and gilt ornamentation, reminiscent of Versailles.

- The Grand Staircase and Bust Gallery, showcasing sculptures of famous composers.

These tours reveal the history and craftsmanship behind one of the world's great opera houses.

Practical Information
Location: Teatro Colón, Cerrito 628, C1010AAN, Buenos Aires, Argentina.
Opening Hours (Guided Tours): Daily from 10:00 a.m. to 5:00 p.m., with tours starting every 15 minutes in Spanish and English. Last entry at 4:30 p.m.
Cost of Access (2026):
Guided Tour: Around ARS 15,000 (USD $18). Discounts available for students, children, and Argentine residents.
Performance Tickets: Prices vary widely depending on the show and seating, ranging from ARS 8,000 (USD $10) in upper galleries to ARS 60,000+ (USD $70+) for premium orchestra seats. Advance booking online is recommended for major productions.
How to Get There:
Subte (Metro): Line D to Tribunales Station, just a 5-minute walk from the theater.
Bus: Lines 24, 29, and 60 stop nearby.
Taxi/Rideshare: Central location makes it accessible within 10 minutes from most downtown hotels.

Traveler Insights & Tips
- **Book Early for Performances** – Tickets for high-profile operas and ballets often sell out weeks in advance. If attending a show is on your list, purchase online as soon as schedules are released.

- **Go for the Tour If You Can't Attend a Show** – The guided tour is comprehensive and allows you to appreciate the theater's beauty even without a performance. Tours in English run frequently.

- **Dress Code** – While there is no strict dress code for performances, locals often dress elegantly, especially for evening shows. Smart-casual attire is recommended to blend in.

- **Combine with Nearby Attractions** – Teatro Colón sits just off Avenida 9 de Julio, the world's widest avenue. After your visit, stroll to the Obelisco, one of Buenos Aires' most famous landmarks, located just a few blocks away.

- **Accessibility** – The theater provides wheelchair access, and headsets are available for guided tours in multiple languages.

Why It Matters to Travelers

Visiting Teatro Colón is more than seeing a theater—it's stepping into Argentina's cultural pride. For history lovers, it showcases the wealth and ambition of Buenos Aires' golden age. For art enthusiasts, it offers a chance to experience one of the world's greatest venues. And for every traveler, whether through a performance or a guided tour, it promises an unforgettable moment in the heart of the city.

La Boca & Caminito Street

The Neighborhood of La Boca

La Boca is one of Buenos Aires' most vibrant and colorful neighborhoods, famous for its artistic spirit, immigrant history, and lively streets. Situated near the old port, it was originally home to Italian immigrants, mainly from Genoa, who built houses from scrap wood and corrugated metal left behind at the docks. To brighten their humble homes, they painted them with leftover ship paint, creating the kaleidoscope of colors that still defines the neighborhood today.

The area has since transformed into a cultural hotspot where art, tango, and football come together. Although parts of La Boca remain working-class and gritty, Caminito Street and its surroundings attract visitors from all over the world eager to experience its unique character.

Caminito Street: The Living Museum
The centerpiece of La Boca is Caminito, a pedestrian street that feels like an open-air museum. Artists display their work, tango dancers perform on the cobblestones, and musicians fill the air with lively rhythms. Every corner bursts with color, from bright murals to the rainbow-painted houses that line the street.

Caminito was officially established as a pedestrian museum in 1959, thanks to artist Benito Quinquela Martín, who grew up in the neighborhood and wanted to preserve its cultural heritage. Today, it remains one of the most photographed places in Buenos Aires, perfect for travelers seeking iconic snapshots of the city.

Art, Tango, and Souvenirs
Street Tango Performances – Expect to see couples dancing the tango in full costume for tips or photos. These shows are informal but authentic glimpses into local tradition.

Local Artisans & Souvenir Stalls – Dozens of stands sell paintings, crafts, leather goods, and tango-themed souvenirs. Prices vary, but bargaining is uncommon.

Murals & Sculptures – Caminito is covered in striking murals depicting Argentine culture, politics, and football. Quirky sculptures of famous figures like Diego Maradona, Evita, and Pope Francis lean from balconies, adding to the fun atmosphere.

Football Culture – Boca Juniors & La Bombonera
Just a few blocks from Caminito lies La Bombonera (Estadio Alberto J. Armando), home to Boca Juniors, one of Argentina's most famous football teams. Football fans should not miss a visit to the stadium or the Boca Juniors Museum, which chronicles the team's history and

showcases trophies, jerseys, and memorabilia. Match days transform the entire neighborhood, with fans filling the streets in blue and yellow.

Practical Information for Caminito Street
Location: Caminito, between Caminito and Del Valle Iberlucea streets, La Boca, C1169 CABA, Buenos Aires, Argentina.
Opening Hours: Open-air street, accessible daily 24/7. However, shops, stalls, and performances are typically active from 10:00 a.m. to 6:00 p.m.
Cost of Access: Free to walk around. Purchases, food, and tips for dancers/performers are at your discretion.
How to Get There:
Bus: Lines 29, 64, and 152 connect the city center with La Boca.
Taxi/Rideshare: A safer and faster option, especially for those unfamiliar with the city.
Subte (Metro): No subway lines reach La Boca directly. The closest is Constitución Station (Line C), followed by a short taxi or bus ride.

Practical Information for La Bombonera (Optional Visit)
Location: Brandsen 805, C1161AAQ, La Boca, Buenos Aires, Argentina.
Opening Hours (Museum & Tours): Daily from 10:00 a.m. to 5:00 p.m. (closed on match days).
Cost of Access (2026): Museum and stadium tour tickets cost around ARS 12,000–18,000 (USD $15–22). Match tickets vary widely depending on the event.
How to Get There: Same as Caminito. Walking from Caminito to the stadium takes about 10 minutes.

Traveler Insights & Tips
- **Safety First** – While Caminito itself is tourist-friendly, surrounding streets in La Boca can be unsafe, especially after dark. Stick to main areas and avoid wandering into residential backstreets.

- **Best Time to Visit** – Go in the morning or early afternoon to see performers and markets at their liveliest. Weekends are especially vibrant.

- **Photography** – Caminito is one of the most photographed areas of Buenos Aires. Be mindful when taking pictures of performers—they often expect a tip in return.

- **Combine with a Football Experience** – If you're a football fan, visiting Caminito and La Bombonera together makes for a memorable half-day itinerary.

- **Food Stops** – Try traditional Argentine dishes at one of the many parrillas (grill restaurants) near Caminito. Expect slightly higher tourist prices, but the atmosphere makes it worthwhile.

Why Travelers Shouldn't Miss It
La Boca and Caminito Street offer a colorful, sensory-packed experience of Buenos Aires. From tango and art to football and history, this neighborhood captures the spirit of the city in one lively district. It's not just about sightseeing—it's about immersing yourself in the heartbeat of Argentine culture.

San Telmo

The Spirit of Old Buenos Aires
San Telmo is one of Buenos Aires' oldest neighborhoods, a district where cobblestone streets, colonial architecture, and bohemian charm create a timeless atmosphere. Once a fashionable residential area for the city's elite in the 18th and early 19th centuries, the neighborhood declined after wealthy families moved north during a yellow fever outbreak in the 1870s. Immigrant communities then settled here, giving San Telmo its eclectic character.

Today, San Telmo is a favorite for travelers who want to experience the authentic and historic side of Buenos Aires. Its leafy plazas, antique shops, tango bars, and crumbling-yet-beautiful mansions make it one of the city's most atmospheric neighborhoods.

San Telmo Market (Mercado de San Telmo)
At the heart of the neighborhood lies the San Telmo Market, a covered marketplace built in 1897. Inside, iron columns and high ceilings frame a maze of stalls selling antiques, artisanal goods, fresh produce, meats, and traditional snacks. Travelers can browse vintage furniture, vinyl records, and rare collectibles, or simply stop for an empanada or choripán at one of the food stalls.
Location: Mercado de San Telmo, Defensa 963, C1065AAU, Buenos Aires, Argentina.
Opening Hours: Daily from 9:00 a.m. to 8:00 p.m., though hours may vary by stall. Best visited midday for full activity.
Cost of Access: Free entry, but purchases vary (antiques range widely in price; food stalls from ARS 3,000–6,000 / USD $4–7 for meals).
How to Get There:

Subte (Metro): Line C to Independencia Station, then a 10-minute walk.
Bus: Lines 29, 152, and 86 stop nearby.
Taxi/Rideshare: 10–15 minutes from Microcentro.

San Telmo Sunday Fair (Feria de San Telmo)
Every Sunday, San Telmo explodes with life during its famous street fair. Beginning in Plaza Dorrego and spilling down Defensa Street for nearly 10 blocks, the fair attracts thousands of visitors looking for antiques, handmade crafts, tango performances, and live music.

Visitors will find everything from silverware and jewelry to books, paintings, and quirky vintage finds. Street performers, including tango dancers and folk musicians, add to the festive spirit. By evening, locals gather at cafés and bars around Plaza Dorrego, giving the day a social, communal finish.
Location: Plaza Dorrego, Defensa 1100, C1065AAO, Buenos Aires, Argentina.

Opening Hours: Every Sunday, from around 10:00 a.m. to 5:00 p.m. (best to arrive before noon to avoid crowds).
Cost of Access: Free to enter and wander. Purchases and tipping performers are optional.
How to Get There: Same as San Telmo Market—easily accessible by bus, Subte, or taxi.

Colonial Architecture & Tango Spirit
Beyond the markets, San Telmo itself is a living museum. Strolling its streets reveals Spanish colonial houses, wrought-iron balconies, and hidden courtyards. Some buildings now house boutique hotels, tango clubs, or art galleries.

San Telmo is also home to tango's underground scene. While La Boca offers tourist-oriented shows, San Telmo hosts traditional milongas—dance halls where locals gather late at night to dance socially. Visitors who want a more authentic tango experience should attend a milonga here, either to watch or take a beginner's class.

Traveler Insights & Tips
- **Timing Your Visit** – Sundays are the liveliest thanks to the Feria de San Telmo, but weekdays are quieter and allow for a more relaxed exploration of the neighborhood's architecture and cafés.

- **Shopping Tips** – Antique prices can be high, especially for rare items. Small crafts and souvenirs, however, are affordable and unique. Cash is preferred by many vendors.

- **Safety Note** – The area is generally safe during the day, especially when crowded on Sundays. However, like all busy markets, keep an eye on your belongings to avoid pickpocketing.

- **Combine with Nearby Sights** – From San Telmo, it's easy to walk to Plaza de Mayo or Puerto Madero. This makes it an excellent stop on a full-day walking itinerary of Buenos Aires.

- **Food & Drink** – San Telmo is packed with traditional parrillas (grill restaurants) and bohemian cafés. Try El Desnivel (Defensa 855) for a budget-friendly steak or Bar Plaza Dorrego (corner of Defensa & Humberto 1º) for a drink with history.

Why Travelers Should Visit
San Telmo offers more than antiques—it is a sensory experience of Buenos Aires' past and present. Between the buzzing Sunday fair, atmospheric tango halls, and colonial streets, travelers will discover why this neighborhood is considered the soul of the city. Whether you're hunting for a keepsake, tasting traditional foods, or simply soaking in the lively atmosphere, San Telmo is a highlight that should not be missed.

Puerto Madero

The Transformation of a Port into a Playground
Puerto Madero is Buenos Aires' youngest and most modern neighborhood, a striking contrast to the colonial streets of San Telmo or the colorful facades of La Boca. Once a decaying dock area, the district underwent a massive urban renewal project in the 1990s. Abandoned warehouses were converted into sleek lofts, restaurants, and offices, while glass skyscrapers rose around the old port. Today, Puerto Madero stands as a symbol of modern Argentina, blending waterfront leisure with business, culture, and luxury living.

Strolling along its wide promenades offers a refreshing escape from the city's busy avenues. The docks, known as diques, are lined with upscale dining, chic bars, luxury hotels, and corporate offices. With its blend of modern design and riverside atmosphere, Puerto Madero has become a

must-see destination for travelers who want to experience Buenos Aires' contemporary side.

Puente de la Mujer (Woman's Bridge)
The most iconic landmark in Puerto Madero is the Puente de la Mujer, a pedestrian suspension bridge designed by Spanish architect Santiago Calatrava. Its sleek white design resembles a couple dancing tango, with the angled mast symbolizing a man and the curved walkway symbolizing a woman. At night, when the bridge is illuminated, it provides one of the city's most photogenic views.

Ecological Reserve (Reserva Ecológica Costanera Sur)
Just steps away from the bustling docks lies the Costanera Sur Ecological Reserve, a massive green space covering more than 865 acres. This urban oasis is home to lagoons, trails, and over 200 species of birds. It's a popular spot for walking, jogging, cycling, or simply escaping the urban noise. Travelers who want to see a quieter, more natural side of Buenos Aires should plan a visit here.

Location: Avenida Tristán Achával Rodríguez 1550, Puerto Madero, Buenos Aires.
Opening Hours: Tuesday to Sunday, 8:00 a.m. to 6:00 p.m. (closed on Mondays). Hours may extend in summer to 7:00 p.m.
Cost of Access: Free.
How to Get There: A short walk from central Puerto Madero. From Plaza de Mayo, it's a 15-minute walk east.

Dining and Nightlife
Puerto Madero is one of the city's top gastronomic hubs. The waterfront is lined with restaurants offering Argentine steak, seafood, and international cuisine. Upscale parrillas like Cabaña Las Lilas (Alicia Moreau de Justo 516) are famous for serving premium cuts of beef, while more casual options include pizzerias and riverside cafés.

At night, the neighborhood transforms into one of Buenos Aires' most sophisticated nightlife districts, with rooftop bars, cocktail lounges, and clubs that cater to a chic crowd.

Museums and Cultural Stops
Faena Art Center – A contemporary art space in a converted mill, featuring installations and exhibitions by local and international artists. Location: Aimé Painé 1169, Puerto Madero.

Fortabat Art Collection – Showcasing works by Argentine masters as well as international names like Andy Warhol. Location: Olga Cossettini 141, Puerto Madero.

Practical Information
Location: Puerto Madero district, centered around Dock 3 and Dock 4, Alicia Moreau de Justo Avenue, C1107AAZ, Buenos Aires.
Opening Hours: The neighborhood itself is open 24/7, but restaurants, museums, and attractions vary in operating hours. Most dining spots open from noon until late at night (midnight or later).

Cost of Access: Free to walk around. Dining, museum entry, or nightlife experiences vary in cost.
Museum Tickets: ARS 5,000–8,000 (USD $6–10) per entry.
Meals: Expect ARS 8,000–15,000 (USD $10–18) per person at mid-range restaurants; luxury dining significantly higher.
How to Get There:
Walking: A 10–15 minute walk east from Plaza de Mayo.
Bus: Lines 4, 20, and 129 stop near Puerto Madero.
Subte (Metro): No direct line; nearest stations are on Line A (Plaza de Mayo) and Line B (Leandro N. Alem), followed by a walk or short taxi ride.
Taxi/Rideshare: Widely available and convenient, especially at night.

Traveler Insights & Tips
- **Best Time to Visit** – Go in the late afternoon, when the light is perfect for photography. Stay into the evening for dinner and views of the skyline lit up at night.

- **Safety** – Puerto Madero is one of the safest districts in Buenos Aires due to its modern development and heavy security presence. Still, keep standard travel precautions in mind.

- **Perfect for Couples** – The romantic riverside walkways, upscale restaurants, and tango-inspired bridge make Puerto Madero ideal for an evening date.

- **Balance Luxury with Budget** – While many restaurants here are high-end, it's possible to enjoy the area affordably by grabbing street food or picnicking near the reserve.

- **Combine with San Telmo** – Puerto Madero sits adjacent to San Telmo, so travelers can easily plan a day exploring colonial history in the morning and modern Buenos Aires by evening.

Why Travelers Should Visit

Puerto Madero captures Buenos Aires' modern face—a neighborhood that combines sleek architecture, cultural venues, luxury dining, and natural escapes. Whether you're walking across the Puente de la Mujer, enjoying a steak by the waterfront, or exploring the ecological reserve, Puerto Madero offers travelers a stylish yet accessible way to experience the city's future alongside its rich past.

Palermo

The Largest and Most Diverse Neighborhood

Palermo is Buenos Aires' largest barrio (neighborhood) and one of its most dynamic. Known for its leafy boulevards, sprawling parks, cultural institutions, and fashionable boutiques, it is a destination that combines relaxation, shopping, and nightlife in one district. Palermo is not just one area but a collection of sub-neighborhoods, each with its own personality:

- **Palermo Soho** – Famous for boutique shopping, design stores, and trendy cafés.

- **Palermo Hollywood** – Known for its bars, nightlife, and restaurants.

- **Palermo Chico** – A quiet, upscale area with embassies and mansions.

- **Palermo Viejo** – Retains a bohemian feel with cobblestone streets and vintage stores.

For travelers in 2026, Palermo is an essential stop, offering both green spaces to unwind and stylish streets that showcase Buenos Aires' cutting-edge culture.

Bosques de Palermo (Palermo Woods)
The Bosques de Palermo, or Palermo Woods, form the city's largest parkland. Spread across nearly 1,000 acres, this collection of parks features lakes, walking paths, rose gardens, and shaded picnic spots. On weekends, locals jog, cycle, rollerblade, and relax here, making it one of the best places to people-watch and join in city life.
Location: Avenida Libertador & Avenida Sarmiento, C1425 CABA, Buenos Aires, Argentina.
Opening Hours: Open daily, 24 hours (though best visited during daylight).
Cost of Access: Free. Boat rentals on the lakes cost around ARS 4,000–6,000 (USD $5–7) per hour.
How to Get There: Subte Line D to Plaza Italia Station, then a 10-minute walk. Buses 10, 34, and 67 also stop nearby.

Jardín Japonés (Japanese Garden)
One of the highlights within Palermo Woods is the Japanese Garden, a gift from the Japanese community in Argentina. It features koi ponds, wooden bridges, bonsai trees, and a serene atmosphere. A small tea house serves traditional Japanese food and green tea.
Location: Av. Casares 3401, C1425CABA, Buenos Aires, Argentina.

Opening Hours: Daily from 10:00 a.m. to 6:00 p.m. (last entry at 5:30 p.m.).
Cost of Access (2026): Around ARS 3,500 (USD $4). Children under 12 enter free.
How to Get There: Subte Line D to Plaza Italia Station, then a 15-minute walk. Taxi or rideshare from central Buenos Aires takes about 20 minutes.

Jardín Botánico (Botanical Garden)

The Carlos Thays Botanical Garden is a peaceful refuge with more than 5,000 plant species from around the world. Its statues, fountains, and Art Nouveau-style greenhouses make it a relaxing place to wander.
Location: Av. Santa Fe 3951, C1425 CABA, Buenos Aires, Argentina.
Opening Hours: Tuesday to Sunday, 9:00 a.m. to 6:00 p.m. Closed Mondays.
Cost of Access: Free.
How to Get There: Subte Line D to Plaza Italia Station – the garden sits right next to the station.

Museo de Arte Latinoamericano de Buenos Aires (MALBA)
Although technically at the edge of Palermo, MALBA is a must for art lovers. The museum features 20th and 21st-century Latin American art, with works by Frida Kahlo, Diego Rivera, and contemporary Argentine artists.
Location: Av. Pres. Figueroa Alcorta 3415, C1425CLA, Buenos Aires, Argentina.
Opening Hours: Thursday to Monday, 12:00 p.m. to 8:00 p.m. Closed Tuesdays.
Cost of Access (2026): ARS 8,000 (USD $10). Discounts for students and seniors. Free entry on Wednesdays.
How to Get There: Subte Line D to Scalabrini Ortiz Station, then a short taxi ride. Buses 130 and 67 also pass nearby.

Palermo Soho & Palermo Hollywood
Beyond its green spaces, Palermo is also Buenos Aires' most fashionable district.

Palermo Soho is filled with indie fashion boutiques, leather shops, bookstores, and cafés with outdoor seating. Murals and street art add to the bohemian charm. Prices vary widely, but visitors can expect to pay around ARS 20,000–35,000 (USD $25–40) for locally designed clothing.

Palermo Hollywood is known for its thriving food and nightlife scene. The area boasts some of the city's trendiest restaurants, cocktail bars, and craft beer breweries. It's especially lively after dark, with spots staying open until the early morning hours.

Traveler Insights & Tips
- **Best Time to Visit Parks** – Early mornings or late afternoons are ideal to enjoy Palermo Woods without the midday heat. Sundays are busy with locals enjoying leisure time.

- **Street Art Lovers** – Palermo Soho and Palermo Hollywood are full of colorful murals. Walking tours are available for around ARS 12,000 (USD $15) per person.

- **Shopping** – Many boutiques in Palermo Soho offer locally designed fashion at higher prices than elsewhere in the city, but the quality and uniqueness make it worthwhile.

- **Food Stops** – Palermo is packed with restaurants for every budget. Try Don Julio (Guatemala 4699) for one of Buenos Aires' best parrillas (steakhouses) – reservations recommended. For a more casual experience, enjoy coffee at Birkin Coffee Bar (Armenia 1640).

- **Nightlife Safety** – Palermo is one of the safest areas at night, but as with any nightlife district, keep an eye on belongings and use rideshares or taxis to return to your hotel late.

Why Travelers Should Visit
Palermo encapsulates the diversity of Buenos Aires in one neighborhood. From sprawling parks and serene gardens to cutting-edge boutiques and buzzing nightlife, it offers something for every type of traveler. Whether you're looking to relax, shop, explore art, or dance the night away, Palermo is a district where Buenos Aires' modern energy and natural beauty come together.

Museo Nacional de Bellas Artes

Argentina's Premier Art Museum
The Museo Nacional de Bellas Artes (MNBA) is the most important art museum in Argentina and one of the finest in South America. Opened in 1896 and relocated to its current building in 1933, the museum houses an extensive collection of more than 12,000 works. It offers visitors an impressive journey through European masters, Latin American artists, and Argentina's own rich artistic tradition.

For travelers, MNBA is not just a gallery—it's a cultural hub that reveals how Argentina's history and identity have been shaped by global and local art.

Collection Highlights

The museum's vast collection covers art from the Middle Ages to the present day, but several pieces stand out as must-sees:

- **European Masters** – Works by Goya, Rembrandt, Rubens, Monet, and Van Gogh. Notably, Monet's "La Seine à Lavacourt" and Goya's "Portrait of the Marquis of Caballero" draw crowds.

- **Argentine Artists** – Paintings by Benito Quinquela Martín, Eduardo Sívori, and Xul Solar showcase the nation's own cultural voices.

- **Latin American Modernism** – Works by Diego Rivera and José Clemente Orozco highlight the region's social and political artistic movements.

- **Sculpture & Decorative Arts** – The museum also houses an impressive collection of classical sculpture replicas and decorative pieces.

Temporary Exhibitions & Programs

In addition to its permanent galleries, MNBA regularly hosts temporary exhibitions that bring international and contemporary art to Buenos Aires. By 2026, the museum has also strengthened its digital platforms, offering QR codes and multilingual audio guides that enhance the visitor experience. Workshops, lectures, and children's programs run throughout the year, making it a destination for families as well as art enthusiasts.

Practical Information

Location: Museo Nacional de Bellas Artes, Av. del Libertador 1473, C1425AAA, Recoleta, Buenos Aires, Argentina.
Opening Hours:
Tuesday to Friday: 11:00 a.m. – 8:00 p.m.
Saturday & Sunday: 10:00 a.m. – 8:00 p.m.
Closed on Mondays and certain national holidays.
Cost of Access (2026): General admission is free. Temporary special exhibitions may charge a fee (typically ARS 4,000–6,000 / USD $5–7).
How to Get There:
Subte (Metro): Line H to Las Heras Station, then a 15-minute walk.
Bus: Lines 17, 61, and 67 all stop near Av. del Libertador.
Taxi/Rideshare: About 10 minutes from the city center (Microcentro).

Traveler Insights & Tips

- **Plan Enough Time** – The museum is large, so allow at least 2–3 hours if you want to explore both European and Argentine collections.

- **Use the Free Entry** – Since general admission is free, it's easy to visit more than once if you're staying in the city longer.

- **Combine with Nearby Attractions** – MNBA is located in Recoleta, making it easy to pair your visit with Recoleta Cemetery, the Floralis Genérica sculpture, or the Recoleta Cultural Center, all within walking distance.

- **Accessibility** – The museum is wheelchair accessible, and guided tours in English and Spanish are often offered for free on weekends.

- **Best Time to Visit** – Mornings on weekdays are quieter, while weekends bring larger crowds, especially when special exhibitions are on display.

Why Travelers Should Visit
The Museo Nacional de Bellas Artes offers travelers a chance to see masterpieces from Europe alongside Argentina's own artistic heritage—without the high ticket prices of other global museums. It's a destination that deepens understanding of Argentine identity and connects the city to the global art world. For art lovers, history enthusiasts, or simply curious travelers, MNBA is one of Buenos Aires' unmissable cultural treasures.

Obelisco & Avenida 9 de Julio

The Symbol of Buenos Aires
The Obelisco de Buenos Aires is the city's most recognizable landmark and an enduring symbol of Argentine identity. Standing 67.5 meters (221 feet) tall, the monument was erected in 1936 to commemorate the

400th anniversary of the first foundation of Buenos Aires. Designed by architect Alberto Prebisch, the Obelisco has since become the backdrop for national celebrations, political rallies, and football victories.

Travelers arriving in Buenos Aires cannot miss it—it dominates the city skyline and sits at the intersection of Avenida 9 de Julio, Avenida Corrientes, and Diagonal Norte, three of the city's busiest avenues. At night, the Obelisco is beautifully illuminated, often in colors representing special events or causes.

Avenida 9 de Julio – The World's Widest Avenue

Running north to south through Buenos Aires, Avenida 9 de Julio is named after Argentina's Independence Day (July 9, 1816). It holds the title of the world's widest avenue, with up to 20 lanes in certain sections. Crossing it on foot can take several minutes, often requiring multiple traffic lights.

The avenue is not just about size—it's also lined with theaters, hotels, cultural centers, and monuments. Walking down Avenida 9 de Julio provides a sweeping introduction to the scale and energy of Buenos Aires.

Nearby Highlights Around the Obelisco
- **Teatro Colón** – Just two blocks away, one of the world's great opera houses.

- **Corrientes Avenue** – Known as the "street that never sleeps," lined with pizzerias, bookshops, and theaters.

- **Plaza de la República** – The plaza where the Obelisco stands, often the site of large gatherings and national celebrations.

- **BA Letters Sign (BA Verde)** – A modern photo spot featuring giant green letters "BA," a popular place for travelers to capture the city's emblem with the Obelisco in the background.

Practical Information
Location: Obelisco de Buenos Aires, Plaza de la República, Av. 9 de Julio & Av. Corrientes, C1043AAB, Buenos Aires, Argentina.
Opening Hours: Open 24/7 as it is located in a public square. Best viewed during the day for activity, or at night when illuminated.
Cost of Access: Free.
How to Get There:
Subte (Metro): Lines B, C, and D all stop at 9 de Julio Station, which exits directly near the Obelisco.
Bus: Numerous city bus lines run along Av. 9 de Julio, including 9, 67, and 100.
Taxi/Rideshare: Easily accessible from anywhere in the city center within 5–10 minutes.

Traveler Insights & Tips
- **Best Time for Photos** – Early morning offers fewer crowds, while evening provides dramatic shots of the illuminated Obelisco against the night sky.

- **Cultural Events** – If visiting during football tournaments or national holidays, expect huge crowds celebrating at the Obelisco. These gatherings are festive but can be overwhelming for some visitors.

- **Safety** – The area is busy and generally safe during the day, but keep an eye on belongings, especially around traffic lights where pickpockets may operate.

- **Combine Attractions** – Pair a visit with Teatro Colón or an evening walk along Corrientes Avenue for a full cultural experience.

- **Street Performances** – On weekends and evenings, expect live music, dancers, and street artists performing near the plaza. Small tips are appreciated.

Why Travelers Should Visit

The Obelisco and Avenida 9 de Julio embody the spirit of Buenos Aires: bold, vibrant, and larger than life. Standing at the heart of the city, the Obelisco is more than just a monument—it's where Argentina gathers to celebrate, mourn, and express its identity. For visitors, it's a perfect spot to start exploring the city's downtown, feel its pulse, and take in one of the most iconic sights in South America.

Day Trip Highlights Nearby

Tigre Delta – A Waterworld Escape from the City

Just 30 kilometers north of Buenos Aires lies the Tigre Delta, a sprawling network of rivers, canals, and islands. Known as the Paraná Delta, it is one of the world's largest deltas, and a favorite weekend retreat for porteños. Life here moves at a slower pace—boats replace cars, waterfront homes dot the riverbanks, and locals sell everything from groceries to ice cream from small motorized launches.

A trip to Tigre gives travelers a chance to experience a completely different side of Buenos Aires: tranquil, green, and water-bound. The town of Tigre itself offers markets, museums, and historic rowing clubs, while boat tours take visitors deeper into the maze of waterways.

Key Attractions in Tigre:
- **Puerto de Frutos** – A bustling riverside market selling crafts, wicker furniture, and regional foods.

- **Mate Museum** – Dedicated to Argentina's national drink, mate, with displays of traditional gourds and bombillas.

- **Boat Tours of the Delta** – Ranging from one-hour excursions to full-day trips, these tours showcase the lifestyle of delta residents and natural beauty of the wetlands.

Practical Information for Tigre:
Location: Tigre, Buenos Aires Province, Argentina (30 km north of the city).
Opening Hours: The town and market are accessible daily; Puerto de Frutos is open from 10:00 a.m. to 7:00 p.m. daily, busiest on weekends. Boat tours typically run from 9:00 a.m. to 6:00 p.m.
Cost of Access:
Train Ticket: ARS 600 (USD $0.70) one-way on the Mitre Line from Retiro to Tigre (2026 rates).
Boat Tours: From ARS 8,000–15,000 (USD $10–18) per person for short tours, up to ARS 30,000 (USD $35) for day-long excursions.
How to Get There:
Train: The Mitre Line departs from Retiro Station in Buenos Aires and arrives in Tigre in about 50 minutes. Address: Retiro Train Station, Av. Ramos Mejía 1430, C1104, Buenos Aires.
Bus: Several long-distance buses connect the city with Tigre, though the train is faster and more scenic.

Taxi/Rideshare: Around 40–50 minutes depending on traffic, costing approximately ARS 20,000–25,000 (USD $24–30).

Traveler Insights for Tigre:
- Weekends are busiest with locals, so weekdays offer a calmer experience.

- Bring cash for small purchases at the market or food stalls.

- Combine a boat trip with a stop at Puerto de Frutos for a full-day outing.

- Ideal for families and couples who want a relaxing contrast to the urban energy of Buenos Aires.

Colonia del Sacramento – A UNESCO Gem Across the River
For those looking to add another country to their trip, Colonia del Sacramento in Uruguay makes for a charming and easy day trip. Founded in 1680 by the Portuguese, this UNESCO World Heritage Site is famous for its cobblestone streets, colonial houses, and riverside sunsets over the Río de la Plata.

Colonia feels worlds away from Buenos Aires' bustling streets. Its historic quarter (Barrio Histórico) is filled with 17th-century buildings, small plazas, and artisan shops. Travelers can climb the lighthouse for panoramic views, stroll along Calle de los Suspiros (Street of Sighs), or enjoy local Uruguayan cuisine in a riverside café.

Key Attractions in Colonia:
- **Barrio Histórico** – The heart of Colonia, with preserved Portuguese and Spanish colonial architecture.

- **Colonia Lighthouse** – Built in 1857, offering sweeping views of the town and river.

- **Museo Portugués & Museo Municipal** – Small but informative museums about Colonia's history.

- **Riverside Promenade** – Perfect for sunset walks and photography.

Practical Information for Colonia del Sacramento:
Location: Colonia del Sacramento, Colonia Department, Uruguay.
Opening Hours: The town is open year-round; museums usually operate Tuesday to Sunday, 11:00 a.m. to 5:00 p.m.
Cost of Access:
Ferry Tickets (Buenos Aires to Colonia): Round-trip tickets with Buquebus, Seacat, or Colonia Express range from ARS 45,000–70,000 (USD $55–85) depending on the season and class. Travel time is about 1 hour.
Museum Tickets: Each museum typically charges ARS 2,000 (USD $2.50), or a combined ticket for several museums is available for about ARS 6,000 (USD $7.50).
How to Get There:
Ferries depart from Puerto Madero Ferry Terminal, Av. Antártida Argentina 821, C1104, Buenos Aires. The trip across the Río de la Plata takes about 1 hour.

Traveler Insights for Colonia:
- Passport and immigration control are required—allow extra time before ferry departure.

- Book ferry tickets in advance, especially during summer (December–February) and weekends.

- Colonia is best explored on foot, but golf carts and bicycles can be rented near the port for ARS 8,000–12,000 (USD $10–15) per day.

- Many travelers choose Colonia as a day trip, but staying overnight in a boutique hotel allows for a quieter experience after day-trippers leave.

Why Travelers Shouldn't Miss These Day Trips
Both Tigre and Colonia del Sacramento offer refreshing contrasts to Buenos Aires. Tigre immerses visitors in Argentina's river culture and natural landscapes, while Colonia adds a cross-border adventure into Uruguay's colonial past. Together, they provide cultural depth and variety, making them two of the best day trip options for travelers looking to extend their Buenos Aires journey.

CHAPTER 3: GETTING THERE & GETTING AROUND

Flights into Ezeiza International Airport (EZE) & Aeroparque Jorge Newbery (AEP)

Buenos Aires is served by two main airports, each catering to different types of travelers.

Ezeiza International Airport (EZE) – Officially known as Ministro Pistarini International Airport, Ezeiza is the primary international gateway to Argentina. Located about 32 km southwest of downtown Buenos Aires, it handles the majority of long-haul flights from Europe, North America, Asia, and Oceania. In 2026, Ezeiza continues to expand with upgraded terminals and faster immigration processes, making arrivals smoother than in the past.

Transport from Ezeiza to the city:

Shuttle Buses: Tienda León offers regular buses to central Buenos Aires (Puerto Madero) for around ARS 15,000 (USD $18). Travel time: 50–60 minutes.

Taxis: Official airport taxis to downtown cost approximately ARS 25,000–30,000 (USD $30–36). Prepaid at counters inside the terminal.

Rideshares: Uber, Cabify, and DiDi operate here with designated pick-up points. Prices are similar to taxis but may vary during peak hours.

Private Transfers: Hotels and travel agencies can arrange private cars for ARS 35,000+ (USD $40+).

Aeroparque Jorge Newbery (AEP) – Located just 7 km from downtown along the Río de la Plata, Aeroparque primarily handles domestic flights and short regional routes (to Uruguay, Brazil, Chile, and Paraguay). For travelers connecting to destinations like Mendoza, Iguazú Falls, or Bariloche, Aeroparque is the most convenient option.

Transport from Aeroparque to the city:
Taxi/Rideshare: Quick and affordable at ARS 6,000–9,000 (USD $7–11).
Bus: Several public buses connect Aeroparque with different parts of the city, including lines 33, 37, 45, and 160. Travel time: 30–45 minutes.

Traveler Insight – If you're arriving internationally, you'll land at Ezeiza. If you're connecting to another Argentine city, expect to transfer to Aeroparque, which takes about an hour by car. Allow at least 4 hours between flights to avoid stress.

Visa & Entry Requirements for 2026

Argentina has simplified entry procedures in recent years to encourage tourism.

- **Visa-Free Access** – Citizens of the EU, UK, USA, Canada, Australia, New Zealand, Japan, and most South American countries do not need a visa for short stays (up to 90 days) for tourism or business purposes.

- **Electronic Travel Authorization (AVE)** – Some nationalities (including travelers from India and China) can apply online for an AVE instead of a traditional visa if they already hold a valid U.S. or Schengen visa. This saves time and reduces paperwork.

- **Traditional Visa** – For travelers outside the visa-free or AVE categories, visas must be obtained from Argentine consulates prior to arrival. Requirements include proof of accommodation, return ticket, financial means, and travel insurance.

- **Passport Validity** – Passports must be valid for at least 6 months beyond your planned departure date from Argentina.

- **Onward/Return Ticket** – Airlines may request proof of onward or return travel at check-in.

- **Travel Insurance** – Not officially required, but strongly recommended, particularly coverage that includes medical care and repatriation.

Traveler Insight – Immigration officers in Buenos Aires airports are generally efficient, but queues can be long during peak hours. Have accommodation details handy, as officials sometimes ask where you are staying.

Public Transportation

Subte (Metro)

The Buenos Aires Subte is the oldest subway system in Latin America, dating back to 1913, and remains the fastest way to get around the city center. It has 6 lines (A, B, C, D, E, H) covering much of the downtown and connecting popular neighborhoods like Palermo, Recoleta, San Telmo, and Microcentro.

Operating Hours: Monday–Saturday 5:30 a.m. – 11:30 p.m., Sundays and holidays 8:00 a.m. – 10:30 p.m.

Cost: A single ride costs around ARS 500 (USD $0.60) with the rechargeable SUBE card. Discounts apply the more you ride in a month.

How to Use: Buy a SUBE card (available at Subte stations, kiosks, and convenience stores) and top it up with cash or card. Tap to enter.

Tip: Avoid rush hours (8:00–10:00 a.m. and 5:00–7:00 p.m.) when trains are crowded.

Buses (Colectivos)

Buenos Aires has an extensive bus network that operates 24/7, reaching places the Subte doesn't. Each bus line is color-coded and numbered.

Cost: Around ARS 500–600 (USD $0.60–0.70) per ride, paid only with a SUBE card. No cash accepted.

Tip: Google Maps and apps like "BA Cómo Llego" are essential for navigating routes.

Taxis

Taxis are plentiful and relatively affordable, especially for short distances. They are black with yellow roofs.

Cost: Base fare is around ARS 1,000 (USD $1.20), with ARS 200 (USD $0.25) per 200 meters. A 15-minute trip within central Buenos Aires typically costs ARS 6,000–8,000 (USD $7–10).

Tip: Always use official taxis—hail them from the street or call radio taxis. Avoid unmarked cars near bus or train stations.

Rideshares (Uber, Cabify, DiDi)

Rideshare apps operate widely in Buenos Aires and are often cheaper than taxis, though payment is usually via credit card through the app. Cabify is especially popular as it uses licensed drivers.

Cost: Similar to taxis or slightly lower, depending on traffic and demand.
Tip: At airports, follow app instructions for designated pick-up zones.

Traveler Insight – Buenos Aires' public transport is cheap and efficient, but learning to use the SUBE card system is key. Keep one card per group, as multiple passengers can tap the same card for rides.

Navigating the City on Foot & Bike

Walking Buenos Aires
Buenos Aires is a walkable city, especially in central districts like Microcentro, Recoleta, Palermo, and San Telmo. Wide boulevards, leafy plazas, and pedestrian-only streets such as Florida Street and Lavalle Street make exploring on foot both practical and enjoyable. Many of the city's top attractions are clustered within walking distance, and strolling through neighborhoods reveals architectural gems, hidden cafés, and vibrant street art.
Distances: Walking from the Obelisco to Recoleta takes about 30 minutes. From San Telmo to Plaza de Mayo is just 10 minutes.
Tips: Wear comfortable shoes, as sidewalks can be uneven in some areas. Summers (December–February) can be hot, so carry water and sunscreen.

Cycling in Buenos Aires
In the past decade, Buenos Aires has invested heavily in becoming a bike-friendly city. The city now has over 250 kilometers of dedicated bike lanes (ciclovías), connecting major neighborhoods. Cycling is a fast, eco-friendly way to see more of the city, especially in Palermo and Puerto Madero.
EcoBici Program: Buenos Aires' public bike-sharing system, available 24/7.
Registration: Free for locals and international visitors via the BA Ecobici app (requires ID or passport).

Cost: The first 1 hour is free for standard users, additional hours cost ARS 1,500–2,000 (USD $2–2.50). Daily and weekly passes are also available for travelers.

Where to Ride: Palermo Woods, Puerto Madero waterfront, and Costanera Sur are safe and scenic cycling routes.

Rentals: Private bike rentals are available in Palermo and San Telmo for ARS 6,000–10,000 (USD $7–12) per day.

Travel Passes & Prepaid Cards (SUBE Card)

SUBE Card – Your Key to Public Transport

The SUBE card (Sistema Único de Boleto Electrónico) is essential for using Buenos Aires' Subte (metro), buses, and trains. Cash is not accepted on public transport.

Where to Get It: SUBE cards can be purchased at Subte stations, kiosks, and official outlets. Cost in 2026: ARS 1,000 (USD $1.20).

How to Recharge: Cards can be reloaded with cash at kiosks or electronically via the "Carga SUBE" app. Machines in metro stations also allow top-ups.

Discounts: The system offers automatic discounts for multiple rides in a day (called the "Red SUBE" system). After the first ride, each transfer within 2 hours costs less.

Coverage: One SUBE card can be used by multiple travelers—just tap once for each person boarding.

Other Travel Passes

For tourists, Buenos Aires has introduced short-term visitor passes that bundle transport and discounts on attractions. The BA Visit Pass, available from 2025, includes unlimited Subte and bus rides for 3, 5, or 7 days plus discounts on museums and guided tours.

Cost (2026): Around ARS 12,000 for 3 days (USD $15), ARS 20,000 for 5 days (USD $24), ARS 28,000 for 7 days (USD $34).

Where to Buy: Airport kiosks, tourist information centers, and online via the BA tourism website.

Safety Tips for Transport

Buenos Aires is generally safe for travelers using transport, but like all big cities, it's best to stay alert and take precautions.

On the Subte (Metro):
Avoid traveling during peak rush hours if possible (8:00–10:00 a.m. and 5:00–7:00 p.m.) when carriages get crowded.

Keep backpacks in front of you and phones out of sight. Pickpocketing can occur in busy stations.

On Buses (Colectivos):
Board using the front door and tap your SUBE card on the machine. Always know your stop in advance, as bus drivers may not announce them.

At night, sit near the driver or avoid buses altogether if unfamiliar with the area.

Taxis & Rideshares:
Use official black-and-yellow taxis or rideshare apps like Uber and Cabify. Avoid unmarked cars around bus or train stations.

Always check that the meter is running in regular taxis.

Walking:
Stick to busy, well-lit streets at night. Avoid walking alone in unfamiliar neighborhoods.

Pedestrian crossings on wide avenues like 9 de Julio may require multiple lights—wait for the green signal as traffic can be aggressive.

Cycling:
Stick to marked bike lanes. Avoid riding at night in poorly lit areas.

Always lock rental bikes securely when unattended.

Traveler Insight – Many locals still prefer cash transactions, so carry small bills and coins for kiosks or SUBE top-ups. Keep valuables secure and avoid displaying expensive cameras or jewelry while using public transport.

CHAPTER 4: ACCOMMODATION IN BUENOS AIRES

Budget Stays

Buenos Aires is very traveler-friendly when it comes to budget accommodation. Hostels and guesthouses here are lively, social, and often located in prime neighborhoods like Palermo, San Telmo, and Microcentro. They're ideal for backpackers, solo travelers, and anyone looking to stretch their budget while still being close to the action.

1. Milhouse Hostel Avenue

Location: Av. de Mayo 1245, C1085ABC, Buenos Aires.
Cost: Dorm beds from ARS 12,000 (USD $14) per night; private rooms from ARS 28,000 (USD $34).
Facilities: Bar, social events, walking tours, free Wi-Fi, 24-hour reception.
Insights: Famous for its party atmosphere and social vibe. Perfect for young travelers who want nightlife and organized activities.

2. America del Sur Hostel Buenos Aires

Location: Chacabuco 718, San Telmo, C1069AAP, Buenos Aires.
Cost: Dorms from ARS 10,000 (USD $12); private rooms from ARS 24,000 (USD $29).
Facilities: Modern design, communal kitchen, lounge, airport transfer services.
Insights: A stylish hostel with a quieter vibe than Milhouse. Great for couples or solo travelers who want comfort on a budget.

3. Art Factory San Telmo

Location: Piedras 545, San Telmo, C1070AAK, Buenos Aires.
Cost: Dorm beds from ARS 9,500 (USD $11); private doubles from ARS 22,000 (USD $27).
Facilities: Rooftop terrace, colorful murals, communal kitchen, live music nights.
Insights: A creative and artsy hostel with a strong community vibe. Its rooftop bar is a favorite among budget travelers.

4. Rayuela Hostel Boutique

Location: Av. Belgrano 887, Monserrat, C1092AAB, Buenos Aires.
Cost: Dorms from ARS 11,000 (USD $13); private rooms from ARS 26,000 (USD $31).
Facilities: Free breakfast, library, shared kitchen, organized excursions.
Insights: Small, family-run hostel with a cozy atmosphere. Ideal for travelers seeking a quieter, homier experience.

5. Che Juan Hostel BA
Location: Lavalle 477, Microcentro, C1047AAE, Buenos Aires.
Cost: Dorm beds from ARS 12,500 (USD $15); private rooms from ARS 27,000 (USD $33).
Facilities: Comfortable beds with privacy curtains, modern décor, free Wi-Fi, kitchen.
Insights: Centrally located near the Obelisco, making it ideal for sightseeing. A good choice for budget travelers who want a mix of socializing and rest.

Mid-Range Options

For those seeking a balance between comfort and affordability, mid-range boutique hotels and serviced apartments are excellent choices in Buenos Aires. Many of these are located in Palermo, Recoleta, and San Telmo, offering stylish design, personalized service, and modern amenities.

1. Mine Hotel Boutique
Location: Gorriti 4770, Palermo Soho, C1414BJL, Buenos Aires.
Cost: Rooms from ARS 65,000 (USD $80) per night.
Facilities: Outdoor pool, garden courtyard, complimentary breakfast, free Wi-Fi.
Insights: A chic boutique hotel in the heart of Palermo Soho's trendy café and shopping scene. Great for couples or design-conscious travelers.

2. CasaSur Recoleta Hotel

Location: Av. Callao 1823, Recoleta, C1024AAA, Buenos Aires.
Cost: Rooms from ARS 70,000 (USD $85) per night.
Facilities: Spa, fitness center, in-house restaurant, room service.
Insights: Stylish and sophisticated, this boutique hotel offers easy access to Recoleta Cemetery and upscale dining.

3. Boutique Suites Palermo

Location: Thames 2313, Palermo, C1425FIG, Buenos Aires.
Cost: Suites from ARS 55,000 (USD $67) per night.
Facilities: Kitchenettes, outdoor pool, rooftop terrace, free breakfast.
Insights: Ideal for longer stays, thanks to kitchen facilities. Surrounded by Palermo's nightlife and shopping.

4. Anselmo Buenos Aires, Curio Collection by Hilton

Location: Don Anselmo Aieta 1069, San Telmo, C1103AAA, Buenos Aires.
Cost: Rooms from ARS 75,000 (USD $92) per night.
Facilities: Fitness center, restaurant, modern design, meeting spaces.

Insights: Combines modern luxury with the old-world charm of San Telmo. Perfect for travelers who want boutique style backed by Hilton standards.

5. IQ Callao by Recoleta Apartments

Location: Av. Callao 1234, Recoleta, C1023AAZ, Buenos Aires.
Cost: Apartments from ARS 60,000 (USD $73) per night.
Facilities: Self-catering apartments, rooftop pool, gym, laundry facilities.
Insights: Great for families or long-stay travelers who want more independence with hotel-level amenities.

Luxury Hotels

Buenos Aires offers some of South America's most refined luxury hotels, blending European-style grandeur with Argentine hospitality. These properties feature world-class dining, spas, and service, making them ideal for travelers seeking comfort and indulgence.

1. Alvear Palace Hotel

Location: Av. Alvear 1891, Recoleta, C1129AAA, Buenos Aires.
Cost: From ARS 200,000 (USD $240) per night.
Facilities: Spa, rooftop pool, fine dining, champagne bar, butler service.
Insights: Opened in 1932, this is Buenos Aires' most iconic luxury hotel, often compared to Europe's finest. Perfect for travelers seeking timeless elegance.

2. Four Seasons Hotel Buenos Aires
Location: Posadas 1086, Retiro, C1011ABB, Buenos Aires.
Cost: From ARS 210,000 (USD $250) per night.
Facilities: Outdoor pool, spa, luxury steakhouse (Elena), bar.
Insights: Combines a modern tower with a 20th-century French mansion. A favorite of international celebrities and business travelers.

3. Palacio Duhau – Park Hyatt Buenos Aires
Location: Av. Alvear 1661, Recoleta, C1014AAA, Buenos Aires.
Cost: From ARS 220,000 (USD $260) per night.
Facilities: Garden courtyard, spa, wine bar, art gallery, indoor pool.
Insights: Housed in a restored neoclassical palace, this hotel blends historic luxury with modern sophistication.

4. Hotel Madero Buenos Aires

Location: Rosario Vera Peñaloza 360, Puerto Madero, C1107CLA, Buenos Aires.
Cost: From ARS 160,000 (USD $190) per night.
Facilities: Rooftop pool, spa, business center, restaurant with panoramic views.
Insights: A contemporary option in the sleek Puerto Madero district, ideal for those who prefer modern luxury near the waterfront.

5. Faena Hotel Buenos Aires
Location: Martha Salotti 445, Puerto Madero, C1107CMB, Buenos Aires.
Cost: From ARS 230,000 (USD $270) per night.
Facilities: Philippe Starck design, Cabaret Room (famous tango show), outdoor pool, luxury spa.
Insights: An avant-garde hotel with dramatic design and nightlife flair. Best for travelers wanting style, entertainment, and exclusivity.

Best Neighborhoods to Stay

Recoleta
Elegant and refined, Recoleta is home to tree-lined avenues, French-inspired architecture, and upscale shops. Staying here offers easy access to Recoleta Cemetery, museums, and luxury hotels.
Best for: Luxury travelers, art lovers, those who want quiet sophistication.

Palermo
Trendy and youthful, Palermo is Buenos Aires' largest neighborhood, divided into sub-areas like Palermo Soho and Palermo Hollywood. Known for its boutiques, restaurants, and nightlife.
Best for: Foodies, shoppers, nightlife seekers, long-stay travelers.

San Telmo
Historic and bohemian, San Telmo charms with cobblestone streets, tango clubs, and antique markets. Accommodation here ranges from boutique hotels to hostels.
Best for: History lovers, bohemian travelers, those seeking authentic local flavor.

Microcentro (Downtown)
The business and financial heart of Buenos Aires, close to landmarks like Plaza de Mayo, the Obelisco, and Avenida Corrientes. Offers easy transport connections and mid-range hotels.
Best for: First-time visitors, short stays, travelers who want to be near major attractions.

Puerto Madero (extra option worth noting)
Though not in the original four, Puerto Madero deserves mention. It's modern, safe, and upscale, with luxury hotels and waterfront dining.
Best for: Couples, luxury travelers, and those wanting a contemporary setting.

CHAPTER 5: FOOD & NIGHTLIFE

Traditional Argentine Cuisine

Argentina is world-famous for its food, and Buenos Aires is the culinary capital where travelers can experience the country's rich gastronomic traditions. At the heart of Argentine cuisine are three classics every visitor must try:

Asado (Argentine Barbecue)

Asado is not just food—it's a ritual. Argentines gather around the parrilla (grill) to cook beef cuts like bife de chorizo (sirloin), vacío (flank steak), and ribs, often accompanied by sausages like chorizo and morcilla (blood sausage). Chimichurri, a garlic and herb sauce, is the essential condiment.

Where to Try: Don Julio (Guatemala 4699, Palermo) is one of the city's top parrillas, ranked among the world's best steakhouses. Expect to pay around ARS 30,000–40,000 (USD $36–48) per person. For a more casual experience, try Parrilla Peña (Rodríguez Peña 682, Recoleta), where a full meal costs closer to ARS 20,000 (USD $24).

Empanadas

These savory pastries, usually filled with beef, chicken, or ham and cheese, are an everyday snack. Each region of Argentina has its own twist—spicy in the north, more savory in Buenos Aires.

Where to Try: La Morada (Tucumán 1331, Microcentro) serves homestyle empanadas for around ARS 2,500 each (USD $3). Chains like El Noble or La Americana offer consistent and affordable options.

Milanesa

Argentina's take on the breaded cutlet (similar to schnitzel) is a staple in homes and restaurants. Milanesa a la napolitana, topped with ham, tomato sauce, and melted cheese, is especially beloved.

Where to Try: El Antojo (Tinogasta 3174, Villa Devoto) is famous for its oversized milanesas that can feed two people for ARS 18,000 (USD $22). In central Buenos Aires, La Continental offers milanesa plates from ARS 12,000 (USD $14).

Traveler Insight: Dinner in Buenos Aires usually starts late—locals rarely eat before 9:00 p.m., and many restaurants are busiest at 10:00 or later. Reservations are recommended for popular parrillas.

Must-Try Street Foods

Buenos Aires' street food culture is vibrant and affordable, offering travelers the chance to taste local flavors without breaking the budget.

1. Choripán – A grilled chorizo sausage served in crusty bread with chimichurri. Sold at parrillas and food stalls across the city. Typical price: ARS 4,000–6,000 (USD $5–7). Try one at the Costanera Sur food stands near Puerto Madero.

2. Bondiola Sandwich – Pork shoulder slow-cooked and served in a sandwich with chimichurri or salsa criolla. A popular late-night snack, especially near football stadiums. Price: ARS 5,000–7,000 (USD $6–8).

3. Fainá with Pizza – A chickpea flour flatbread often eaten on top of a slice of pizza ("pizza a caballo"). It's a quirky but beloved Buenos Aires tradition. Try it at Pizzería Güerrín (Av. Corrientes 1368). Price: ARS 3,500 (USD $4) per portion.

4. Tortas Fritas – Fried dough pastries eaten during rainy days or with mate. Sold at bakeries and sometimes from street vendors. Price: ARS 2,500 (USD $3) each.

5. Helado (Ice Cream) – Buenos Aires has a thriving Italian-style gelato scene, with shops offering flavors like dulce de leche, Malbec wine sorbet, and traditional chocolate. Heladería Cadore (Av. Corrientes 1695) is a classic choice. Prices start around ARS 4,000 (USD $5) for two scoops.

Traveler Insight: Street food stalls are busiest at lunch and after football matches. Many operate late into the night, making them a perfect option after bars or tango shows.

Cafés & Historic Coffee Houses

Café culture in Buenos Aires is part of daily life. Porteños spend hours sipping coffee, reading, or debating politics in cafés that are as much social institutions as places to drink. Some cafés are even officially recognized as "bares notables", historic establishments that preserve cultural heritage.

1. Café Tortoni

Location: Av. de Mayo 825, Monserrat, C1084AAA, Buenos Aires.
Hours: Daily, 8:00 a.m. – 10:00 p.m.
Cost: Coffee around ARS 3,500 (USD $4); pastries ARS 2,500 (USD $3).
Insights: Founded in 1858, Café Tortoni is the most famous café in Argentina. Known for its stained glass, wood-paneled walls, and live tango shows.

2. Las Violetas
Location: Av. Rivadavia 3899, Almagro, C1204AAD, Buenos Aires.
Hours: Daily, 8:00 a.m. – midnight.

Cost: Coffee and pastries ARS 6,000 (USD $7) per person.
Insights: A Belle Époque café with chandeliers and marble columns. Their "merienda" (afternoon tea with pastries) is legendary.

3. Café de los Angelitos

Location: Av. Rivadavia 2100, Balvanera, C1033AAX, Buenos Aires.
Hours: Daily, 8:00 a.m. – midnight.
Cost: Coffee around ARS 4,000 (USD $5). Dinner and tango shows available from ARS 50,000 (USD $60).
Insights: Famous for its tango heritage, once frequented by poets, musicians, and politicians.

4. El Gato Negro
Location: Av. Corrientes 1669, San Nicolás, C1042AAC, Buenos Aires.
Hours: Daily, 9:00 a.m. – 11:00 p.m.
Cost: Specialty coffees and teas from ARS 3,500 (USD $4).
Insights: Established in 1927, this café specializes in spices, teas, and exotic coffee blends. A sensory experience unlike any other.

5. La Biela

Location: Av. Quintana 596, Recoleta, C1129AAL, Buenos Aires.
Hours: Daily, 8:00 a.m. – 2:00 a.m.
Cost: Coffee and pastries ARS 5,500 (USD $6).
Insights: A Recoleta institution with outdoor seating under centuries-old rubber trees. Popular with intellectuals, writers, and locals alike.

Traveler Insight: In Buenos Aires, ordering just a coffee often comes with a small cookie, chocolate, or even sparkling water at no extra cost. Take time to linger—cafés are designed for conversation and people-watching, not quick takeaways.

Fine Dining & Michelin-Listed Restaurants

Buenos Aires is not only about parrillas and empanadas—it has emerged as one of Latin America's top fine-dining destinations. In 2023, the Michelin Guide debuted in Argentina, and by 2026, several Buenos Aires restaurants hold stars and recommendations, showcasing innovation alongside tradition.

1. Don Julio (Michelin Star)
Location: Guatemala 4699, Palermo, C1414BJL, Buenos Aires.
Hours: Daily, 12:00 p.m. – 4:00 p.m., 7:00 p.m. – midnight.
Cost: Tasting menu around ARS 55,000 (USD $65).
Insights: Ranked among the World's 50 Best Restaurants, Don Julio elevates Argentine beef into fine art, while maintaining a warm, authentic parrilla feel.

2. El Preferido de Palermo (Michelin Star)
Location: Jorge Luis Borges 2108, Palermo, C1425FUM, Buenos Aires.
Hours: Daily, 12:00 p.m. – 12:30 a.m.
Cost: ARS 30,000–40,000 (USD $36–48) per person.
Insights: A reimagined neighborhood bodega serving classics like milanesa and pickled dishes with a gourmet twist. Its pastel-pink façade is iconic.

3. Aramburu (Two Michelin Stars)
Location: Pasaje del Correo, Vicente López 1661, Recoleta, C1018ABA, Buenos Aires.
Hours: Tuesday–Saturday, 7:00 p.m. – 11:30 p.m.
Cost: Tasting menu ARS 90,000 (USD $110), wine pairing extra.
Insights: A modern gastronomic experience with 18-course tasting menus featuring Argentine ingredients presented with avant-garde techniques.

4. Chila (Michelin Star)
Location: Alicia Moreau de Justo 1160, Puerto Madero, C1107AAX, Buenos Aires.
Hours: Tuesday–Saturday, 7:30 p.m. – midnight.
Cost: Tasting menu ARS 75,000 (USD $90).
Insights: Known for its riverside setting and contemporary Argentine cuisine, Chila is a romantic choice for special nights out.

5. Tegui (Michelin Recommended)
Location: Costa Rica 5852, Palermo, C1414BTG, Buenos Aires.
Hours: Wednesday–Saturday, 7:30 p.m. – 11:00 p.m.
Cost: Tasting menu ARS 70,000 (USD $85).
Insights: Hidden behind a graffiti-covered façade, Tegui offers one of the city's most intimate fine-dining experiences.
Traveler Insight: Reservations are essential for Michelin-starred restaurants, often weeks in advance. Dining experiences are long (2–3 hours), making them ideal for relaxed evenings.

Wine & Malbec Culture

Argentina is synonymous with wine, and Buenos Aires is the perfect place to explore its celebrated Malbec culture without leaving the capital. While Mendoza is the country's wine-producing heartland, the city offers countless wine bars, tasting rooms, and restaurants that highlight Argentina's best vintages.

Malbec – The star of Argentine wine. Expect bold reds with deep fruit flavors, particularly from Mendoza.

Torrontés – A fragrant white wine from Salta, excellent for pairing with lighter meals.

Patagonian Wines – Cooler climate varietals like Pinot Noir and Chardonnay are increasingly popular.

Where to Experience Wine in Buenos Aires:
1. Pain et Vin (Gorriti 5132, Palermo) – A cozy wine bar with curated selections and tastings led by sommeliers. Tastings from ARS 12,000 (USD $14).

2. Vico Wine Bar (Gurruchaga 1149, Villa Crespo) – Offers 18+ wines by the glass using a self-serve dispenser system. Glasses from ARS 2,500 (USD $3).

3. Anuva Wines (Palermo) – Hosts guided tastings of boutique Argentine wines paired with small bites. Tastings ARS 25,000 (USD $30).

4. Aldo's Vinoteca & Restorán (Moreno 372, Monserrat) – A restaurant with an extensive wine list and sommeliers to guide pairings. Bottles from ARS 12,000 (USD $14).

5. Lo de Joaquín Alberdi (JA!) (Jorge Luis Borges 1772, Palermo Soho) – A legendary wine shop that hosts tastings and sells premium bottles to take home.

Traveler Insight: Wine is very affordable compared to Europe or the US. A good bottle in a restaurant costs ARS 10,000–15,000 (USD $12–18). Many venues allow you to purchase bottles directly after tastings.

Nightlife: Tango Shows, Clubs & Bars

Buenos Aires is a city that never sleeps, and its nightlife is as legendary as its food. From traditional tango performances to modern nightclubs and cocktail bars, the city offers something for every taste.

Tango Shows
El Querandí (Perú 302, San Telmo): Intimate tango dinner show in a restored 1920s mansion. Tickets from ARS 55,000 (USD $65) including dinner.

Café de los Angelitos (Av. Rivadavia 2100, Balvanera): Historic café with elegant tango performances. Tickets from ARS 50,000 (USD $60).

- **Señor Tango (Vieytes 1655, Barracas):** Large-scale, theatrical tango show with live horses and special effects. Tickets from ARS 60,000 (USD $72).

- **La Ventana (Balcarce 425, San Telmo):** Combines tango and folk music in an authentic setting. Tickets from ARS 52,000 (USD $62).

- **Rojo Tango at Faena Hotel (Martha Salotti 445, Puerto Madero):** Exclusive luxury tango show in a cabaret-style venue. Tickets from ARS 95,000 (USD $115).

Clubs

Nightclubs in Buenos Aires open late (after midnight) and run until dawn. Palermo Hollywood and Puerto Madero are hotspots.

- **Crobar (Av. Libertador 3886, Palermo):** One of the city's top electronic music clubs. Entry around ARS 20,000 (USD $24).

- **Niceto Club (Niceto Vega 5510, Palermo):** Known for its eclectic music nights, from rock to hip-hop to cumbia. Entry ARS 15,000 (USD $18).

- **Club 69 at Niceto (Thursday nights):** A flamboyant blend of drag, dance, and party culture.

Bars

Buenos Aires also has a thriving cocktail culture, with speakeasies and rooftop bars popular among locals and travelers.

- **Florería Atlántico (Arroyo 872, Retiro):** Consistently ranked among the World's 50 Best Bars. Hidden behind a florist shop. Cocktails from ARS 8,000 (USD $10).

- **Presidente Bar (Av. Pres. Manuel Quintana 188, Recoleta):** Stylish cocktail bar with inventive drinks.

- **Uptown (Arévalo 2030, Palermo Hollywood):** Subway-station-themed bar with DJs and cocktails. Entry is free; cocktails from ARS 7,500 (USD $9).

Traveler Insight: Porteños start nightlife late—tango shows at 9:00 p.m., bars at 11:00 p.m., clubs after 1:00 a.m. Don't plan an early morning the next day if you want to experience Buenos Aires after dark!

CHAPTER 6: SHOPPING & LOCAL MARKETS

Souvenirs Worth Bringing Home

Buenos Aires offers unique souvenirs that reflect Argentina's culture, from tango to gaucho traditions. Popular items include:

Mate Sets – Traditional gourds with bombillas (metal straws), starting around ARS 8,000 (USD $10) for basic sets, sold in markets and shops across the city.

Alfajores – Sweet sandwich cookies filled with dulce de leche, available from ARS 2,500 (USD $3) per pack at bakeries or chains like Havanna.

Wine & Malbec – A good bottle of Argentine Malbec costs ARS 10,000–15,000 (USD $12–18) in shops. Lo de Joaquín Alberdi (Borges 1772, Palermo Soho) is a well-known wine store.

Tango Music & Art – Tango-themed posters, CDs, and vinyl are sold at San Telmo and artisan fairs, starting from ARS 6,000 (USD $7).

Leather Goods – Belts, wallets, and jackets made from Argentine leather are world-renowned. Prices vary: belts from ARS 12,000 (USD $14), jackets from ARS 90,000 (USD $105).

Traveler Insight: Avoid buying souvenirs near top attractions like Caminito, where items are overpriced. Markets and artisan fairs usually offer better deals and quality.

Feria de San Telmo (Antique Market)

The San Telmo Sunday Fair is Buenos Aires' most famous street market, stretching down Defensa Street from Plaza Dorrego. It's a mix of antique treasures, artisan crafts, vintage goods, and lively street performances.
Location: Plaza Dorrego, Defensa 1100, San Telmo, C1065AAO, Buenos Aires.
Opening Hours: Sundays, 10:00 a.m. – 5:00 p.m. (arrive early to avoid crowds).
Cost of Access: Free to enter; prices vary widely for purchases (from ARS 2,000 for trinkets to ARS 200,000+ for antiques).
How to Get There:
Subte (Metro): Line C to Independencia Station, then a 10-minute walk.
Bus: Lines 29, 64, 152 stop near Plaza Dorrego.
Taxi/Rideshare: Around 10 minutes from Microcentro.

Traveler Insights:
- Bargaining is possible for antiques but less common for crafts.
- Keep valuables close—pickpocketing can occur in crowded sections.

- Stay for live tango performances in Plaza Dorrego during the afternoon.

Palermo Soho & Palermo Hollywood Boutiques

Palermo has become Buenos Aires' trendiest shopping hub, particularly in Palermo Soho (around Plaza Serrano) and Palermo Hollywood. Here, independent designers sell clothing, jewelry, and home décor, often with a quirky or bohemian flair.

Location: Around Plaza Serrano (Plaza Cortázar), Honduras 4900, Palermo, C1414BMC, Buenos Aires.

Opening Hours: Shops generally open late, from 11:00 a.m. – 8:00 p.m. daily, with longer hours on weekends.

Cost: Locally designed clothing from ARS 25,000–40,000 (USD $30–48); artisan jewelry from ARS 10,000 (USD $12).

How to Get There:

Subte (Metro): Line D to Plaza Italia Station, then a 15-minute walk.

Bus: Lines 39, 55, 111 serve Palermo.

Traveler Insights:

- Shops are closed during siesta hours in some areas (2:00–4:00 p.m.).

- Many boutiques accept credit cards, but small artisan stands may prefer cash.

- Palermo also features street art, cafés, and nightlife, making it a great all-day destination.

Leather Goods, Crafts, and Art

Argentina is globally known for its leather, and Buenos Aires offers countless shops specializing in handcrafted products. In addition, artisan fairs showcase local crafts and contemporary art.

Murillo Street Leather District (Villa Crespo, Murillo 500–900): Dozens of leather shops selling jackets, handbags, and shoes at lower prices than Recoleta boutiques. Jackets start from ARS 80,000 (USD $95).

Recoleta Handicraft Fair (Plaza Francia, Recoleta): Open weekends from 10:00 a.m. – 6:00 p.m., offering handmade jewelry, crafts, and artwork. Entry free. Address: Av. del Libertador & Av. Pueyrredón, C1118AAE, Buenos Aires.

Galería Patio del Liceo (Av. Santa Fe 2729, Recoleta): A creative hub with small studios and galleries selling contemporary art and design pieces. Entry free.

Usina del Arte (Agustín Caffarena 1, La Boca): Hosts rotating art exhibitions, often free entry, showcasing Argentine and Latin American artists. Open Tue–Sun, 2:00 p.m. – 8:00 p.m.

San Telmo Antique Shops (along Defensa Street, San Telmo): Open daily, with permanent antique shops complementing the Sunday fair.

Traveler Insight: Buy leather goods from reputable stores and request authenticity certificates. Bargains exist in Villa Crespo but expect less variety in styles.

Shopping Malls & Modern Retail

For a modern retail experience, Buenos Aires has shopping malls that combine local and international brands with dining and entertainment.

1. Galerías Pacífico
Location: Florida 753, Microcentro, C1005AAO, Buenos Aires.
Hours: Daily, 10:00 a.m. – 9:00 p.m.
Cost: Free entry; mid- to high-end shopping.
Insights: Famous for its Italian Renaissance-style architecture and frescoed ceilings. Houses fashion brands, leather shops, and art galleries.

2. Alto Palermo Shopping
Location: Av. Santa Fe 3253, Palermo, C1425BGK, Buenos Aires.
Hours: Daily, 10:00 a.m. – 10:00 p.m.
Insights: Trendy mall with clothing stores, tech shops, and a modern food court. Popular among young locals.

3. Dot Baires Shopping
Location: Vedia 3626, Saavedra, C1430DAF, Buenos Aires.
Hours: Daily, 10:00 a.m. – 10:00 p.m.
Insights: One of the largest malls, with international brands, a cinema complex, and dining options.

4. Patio Bullrich
Location: Posadas 1245, Retiro, C1011ABW, Buenos Aires.
Hours: Daily, 10:00 a.m. – 9:00 p.m.
Insights: An upscale mall with luxury brands, located in a restored 19th-century building. Best for high-end shopping.

5. Abasto Shopping
Location: Av. Corrientes 3247, Balvanera, C1193AAA, Buenos Aires.
Hours: Daily, 10:00 a.m. – 10:00 p.m.
Insights: A historic building tied to tango legend Carlos Gardel. Offers mainstream shopping plus family entertainment.

Traveler Insight: Shopping malls are safe and air-conditioned, making them ideal in hot summers. For bargains, look out for mid-season sales (January and July).

CHAPTER 7: ITINERARIES

3-Day Itinerary

Perfect for travelers with limited time who want to experience Buenos Aires' essentials.

Day 1: Historic Core & Tango
Morning: Visit Plaza de Mayo, Casa Rosada, and Metropolitan Cathedral (free entry).
Afternoon: Walk along Avenida de Mayo, stop at Café Tortoni for coffee. Continue to Obelisco & Avenida 9 de Julio.
Evening: Dinner at Don Julio in Palermo (ARS 35,000 / USD $42 pp). Optional tango show at El Querandí (ARS 55,000 / USD $65 with dinner).
Estimated Cost: USD $80–100 including dinner and show.

Day 2: Recoleta & Palermo
Morning: Explore Recoleta Cemetery (ARS 5,000 / USD $6), including Eva Perón's tomb.
Afternoon: Visit Museo Nacional de Bellas Artes (free), then walk to Floralis Genérica sculpture.
Evening: Head to Palermo Soho for boutique shopping and dinner.
Estimated Cost: USD $30–40.

Day 3: San Telmo & La Boca
Morning: Wander through San Telmo Market (Sunday is best).
Afternoon: Explore La Boca & Caminito Street. Optional visit to Fundación Proa Art Museum (ARS 6,000 / USD $7).
Evening: Dinner at a parrilla in San Telmo or Puerto Madero waterfront.
Estimated Cost: USD $40–50.

5-Day Itinerary

Ideal for travelers who want to blend museums, neighborhoods, and leisurely experiences.

Day 1: City Center
Explore Plaza de Mayo, Casa Rosada, Avenida de Mayo.
Afternoon shopping on Florida Street & Galerías Pacífico Mall.
Dinner near Puerto Madero waterfront.

Day 2: Recoleta
Morning: Visit Recoleta Cemetery and surrounding cultural sites.
Afternoon: Museums – MNBA and MALBA (ARS 8,000 / USD $10).
Evening: Wine tasting at Vico Wine Bar (ARS 12,000 / USD $14).

Day 3: Palermo Parks & Nightlife
Morning: Bosques de Palermo (free), Japanese Garden (ARS 3,500 / USD $4).
Afternoon: Botanical Garden & Palermo Soho boutiques.
Evening: Dinner in Palermo, followed by cocktails at Florería Atlántico.

Day 4: San Telmo & La Boca
Morning: Antique shopping in San Telmo, Sunday market if possible.
Afternoon: Caminito Street, tango dancers, Boca Juniors stadium tour (ARS 12,000 / USD $14).
Evening: Dinner & tango show at La Ventana (ARS 52,000 / USD $62).

Day 5: Modern Buenos Aires
Morning: Puerto Madero's Puente de la Mujer & Costanera Sur Ecological Reserve (free).
Afternoon: Visit Faena Art Center or shopping at Patio Bullrich Mall.
Evening: Relax with dinner at El Preferido de Palermo (ARS 30,000 / USD $36 pp).

Estimated Cost: USD $350–450 for 5 days (mid-range, excluding hotels).

7-Day Itinerary

Best for travelers who want to go beyond city highlights and explore the region.

Day 1: Historic Core
Plaza de Mayo, Casa Rosada, Avenida de Mayo, Café Tortoni, Obelisco.

Day 2: Recoleta & Museums
Recoleta Cemetery, MNBA, MALBA, Floralis Genérica. Evening wine tasting.

Day 3: Palermo
Palermo Woods, Japanese Garden, Botanical Garden. Afternoon in Palermo Soho & Hollywood. Nightlife in Palermo.

Day 4: San Telmo & La Boca
San Telmo antiques, San Telmo Market, Caminito, Boca Juniors stadium. Evening tango at Café de los Angelitos.

Day 5: Puerto Madero & Modern Buenos Aires
Walk along the waterfront, visit the Woman's Bridge, Costanera Sur Ecological Reserve. Afternoon: Museo Fortabat. Evening: Fine dining at Chila (ARS 75,000 / USD $90 tasting menu).

Day 6: Tigre Delta Day Trip
Morning: Train from Retiro (50 min, ARS 600 / USD $0.70).
Explore Puerto de Frutos market, boat tour (ARS 10,000 / USD $12).
Afternoon: Mate Museum, riverside lunch.
Evening: Return to Buenos Aires.
Total cost: USD $20–30.

Day 7: Colonia del Sacramento, Uruguay (Day Trip)
Ferry from Puerto Madero (1 hr, ARS 45,000–70,000 / USD $55–85 roundtrip).
Explore UNESCO-listed historic quarter, Colonia Lighthouse, Calle de los Suspiros.
Evening return to Buenos Aires.
Total cost: USD $80–100.

Estimated Cost: USD $600–750 for 7 days (mid-range, excluding hotels).

Traveler Insight: Buenos Aires rewards slow travel. Even with 7 days, you'll still feel there's more to see. Balance walking tours, museums, and nightlife with day trips to make the most of your stay.

CHAPTER 8: HIDDEN GEMS OF BUENOS AIRES

Neighborhoods Off the Beaten Path

Chacarita Cemetery

This sprawling necropolis covers nearly 230 acres, making it Argentina's largest cemetery. Unlike Recoleta, which is ornate and touristy, Chacarita feels raw and authentic. The wide avenues of mausoleums are less polished but deeply atmospheric. It's most famous as the resting place of tango idol Carlos Gardel, where locals often leave flowers, cigars, or even small bottles of whiskey. The cemetery also holds artists, actors, and political figures from Argentina's cultural history.
Location: Av. Guzmán 680, Chacarita, C1414DNP.
Hours: Daily, 7:30 a.m.–5:00 p.m.
Cost: Free.
How to Get There: Subte Line B to Federico Lacroze Station, then a 5-minute walk.

Villa Crespo Leather District (Murillo Street)

Villa Crespo is often overshadowed by trendy Palermo next door, but on Murillo Street you'll find dozens of family-owned leather shops selling belts, jackets, shoes, and handbags at much lower prices than Recoleta or Puerto Madero. Most are factory outlets, meaning you can custom-fit or order pieces in unusual colors. Bargaining is acceptable if you buy more than one item.

Location: Murillo 500–900, Villa Crespo.
Hours: Monday–Saturday, 10:00 a.m.–7:00 p.m.
Cost: Free to browse; jackets from ARS 80,000 (USD $95).
How to Get There: Subte Line B to Malabia Station, then a 10-minute walk.

Patio de los Lecheros

Once a milk distribution hub, this open-air food court has been reborn as one of Buenos Aires' coolest foodie hangouts. It features street food stalls selling Argentine staples (choripán, provoleta cheese, empanadas) alongside international flavors like ramen, tacos, and craft burgers. In

the evenings, live DJs and bands set the atmosphere under string lights. It's beloved by young locals and perfect for travelers who want an offbeat dining experience.
Location: Donato Álvarez 175, Caballito, C1405BMC.
Hours: Wednesday–Sunday, 6:00 p.m.–midnight.
Cost: Free entry; meals ARS 8,000–15,000 (USD $10–18).
How to Get There: Subte Line A to Primera Junta Station, then a 10-minute walk.

Chacarita & Villa Crespo Street Art Circuit

While Palermo gets all the attention for murals, Chacarita and Villa Crespo have become hotbeds for cutting-edge urban art. Gigantic murals adorn factory walls and apartment blocks, including pieces by international artists like Martin Ron. Unlike Palermo, you won't be jostling with tourists—most people here are locals on their way home from work. A guided street art tour adds context about Argentina's politics and culture hidden within the paintings.
Location: Around Av. Corrientes & Av. Dorrego.
Hours: Accessible 24/7.
Cost: Free. Guided tours ARS 12,000 (USD $14).
How to Get There: Subte Line B to Dorrego Station.

Parque Centenario

This massive oval-shaped park in Caballito is a local secret for relaxation. During weekdays it's a peaceful green space where families stroll, joggers circle the pond, and readers laze under shady trees. On weekends, an artisan fair sets up stalls selling crafts, books, and antiques. It feels authentically porteño—very few tourists make it here.
Location: Av. Díaz Vélez 4800, Caballito, C1414CQP.
Hours: Daily, 6:00 a.m.–9:00 p.m.
Cost: Free.
How to Get There: Subte Line A to Acoyte Station, then a 12-minute walk.

Secret Rooftop Bars & Cafés

Trade Sky Bar

Perched atop the historic Comega Building, this stylish rooftop offers breathtaking 360-degree views of the city skyline and Río de la Plata. The bar is spread across multiple levels, with outdoor terraces and indoor lounges. Cocktails lean toward classics with Argentine twists, such as Malbec-infused negronis. It's popular with professionals after work but still under the radar for most tourists.
Location: Av. Corrientes 222, Microcentro, C1043AAP.
Hours: Daily, 6:00 p.m.–2:00 a.m.
Cost: Cocktails ARS 9,000–12,000 (USD $11–14).
How to Get There: Subte Line B to Florida Station.

Salvaje Bakery Rooftop

Salvaje is known for its sourdough and artisanal breads, but few visitors know it has a rooftop terrace hidden above its Palermo location. The rooftop offers a relaxed vibe, perfect for morning coffee or

brunch with friends. Its pastries, especially medialunas (sweet croissants), are among the best in the city.
Location: Av. Dorrego 1829, Palermo, C1414CNP.
Hours: Daily, 8:00 a.m.–8:00 p.m.
Cost: Coffee ARS 3,500 (USD $4), pastries ARS 2,500 (USD $3).
How to Get There: Subte Line D to Palermo Station, then 12-minute walk.

Alvear Roof Bar
One of Buenos Aires' most elegant rooftops, the Alvear Roof Bar combines luxurious cocktails with sophisticated views over Recoleta. Guests enjoy gourmet tapas alongside expertly crafted cocktails while watching the sun set behind the mansions of Recoleta. Dress codes are smart-casual, reflecting the hotel's old-world charm.
Location: Av. Alvear 1891, Recoleta, C1129AAA.
Hours: Daily, 6:00 p.m.–midnight.
Cost: Cocktails from ARS 11,000 (USD $13).
How to Get There: Bus 10, 17, 67 stop nearby.

Ninina Rooftop

This Villa Urquiza café is a hidden suburban gem. The rooftop terrace is bright, with views over a low-rise neighborhood rather than skyscrapers, giving it a cozy, local feel. Their brunch menu—avocado toast, fresh juices, cakes—is especially popular with young locals. Perfect for those wanting to escape Palermo's busyness.
Location: Holmberg 2464, Villa Urquiza, C1430FDT.
Hours: Daily, 9:00 a.m.–10:00 p.m.
Cost: Brunch ARS 12,000–15,000 (USD $14–18).
How to Get There: Subte Line B to Juan Manuel de Rosas Station.

Hotel Pulitzer Sky Bar

Hidden above a boutique hotel near Plaza San Martín, this rooftop attracts a cool, cosmopolitan crowd. On weekends, DJs spin electronic sets while bartenders mix creative cocktails. Despite being centrally located, it retains a secret vibe, with no obvious street advertising.
Location: Maipú 907, Microcentro, C1006ACM.
Hours: Thursday–Saturday, 6:00 p.m.–2:00 a.m.

Cost: Cocktails ARS 8,500–10,500 (USD $10–12).
How to Get There: Subte Line C to San Martín Station.

Little-Known Museums & Street Art Spots
Museo Xul Solar

Dedicated to Argentina's most eccentric artist, this museum showcases Xul Solar's surreal paintings, sculptures, and "invented languages." His visionary works mix mysticism, futurism, and Latin American identity. The museum is housed in his former residence, creating an intimate setting.
Location: Laprida 1212, Recoleta, C1425EFD.
Hours: Tuesday–Sunday, 12:00 p.m.–7:00 p.m.
Cost: ARS 6,000 (USD $7).
How to Get There: Subte Line D to Agüero Station, 10-minute walk.

Museo del Humor (MUHU)
A light-hearted museum featuring Argentine comic art, political cartoons, and children's characters. It appeals to both adults and kids,

showing how humor reflects Argentina's social struggles. Its location in Puerto Madero makes it easy to pair with a waterfront walk.
Location: Av. de los Italianos 851, Puerto Madero, C1107.
Hours: Wed–Sun, 11:00 a.m.–6:00 p.m.
Cost: ARS 5,000 (USD $6).
How to Get There: Bus 4 or 20 to Costanera Sur.

Museo del Títere (Puppet Museum)
Quirky and charming, this small museum features puppets from Argentina and around the world, including traditional marionettes, shadow puppets, and modern creations. Perfect for families and offbeat travelers.
Location: Piedras 905, San Telmo, C1070AAT.
Hours: Sat–Sun, 3:00 p.m.–7:00 p.m.
Cost: ARS 4,000 (USD $5).
How to Get There: Subte Line C to San Juan Station, 5-minute walk.

Colección Fortabat

A sleek, modern museum showcasing the private art collection of Amalia Lacroze de Fortabat. Visitors can see works by Andy Warhol, Turner, and Argentine artists like Antonio Berni. Its riverside location in Puerto Madero adds to the experience.
Location: Olga Cossettini 141, Puerto Madero, C1107CAA.
Hours: Tue–Sun, 12:00 p.m.–8:00 p.m.
Cost: ARS 8,000 (USD $10).
How to Get There: Subte Line B to Leandro N. Alem, then a 15-minute walk.

Barracas Street Art District
Barracas is an industrial neighborhood turned open-air gallery, home to one of the largest murals in Latin America, "El Regreso de Quinquela," covering over 2,000 square meters. Walking here feels like stepping into a giant canvas, with every wall telling a story.
Location: Av. Montes de Oca & Av. Suarez, Barracas.
Hours: Accessible 24/7.
Cost: Free. Tours ARS 15,000 (USD $18).
How to Get There: Bus 24 or 59 to Montes de Oca y Suárez.

Hidden Tango Milongas
La Catedral Club
This alternative tango space feels more like a bohemian art squat than a dance hall. The mismatched furniture, dim red lighting, and enormous warehouse setting create an unforgettable vibe. Beginners are welcome—many come for lessons before the milonga starts.
Location: Sarmiento 4006, Almagro, C1197AAH.
Hours: Daily, 8:00 p.m.–4:00 a.m.
Cost: Entry ARS 6,000 (USD $7); classes ARS 8,000 (USD $10).

El Beso
One of Buenos Aires' most traditional milongas, where tango etiquette is strictly observed. Men invite women with a "cabeceo" (a nod across

the room). The intimate dance floor means you're up close with the passion of tango.
Location: Riobamba 416, Balvanera, C1025ABH.
Hours: Tue–Sun, from 8:00 p.m.
Cost: ARS 7,000 (USD $8).

Salón Canning
Classic wooden floors, mirrored walls, and live tango orchestras make this one of the most authentic milongas in Buenos Aires. It attracts serious dancers but also welcomes curious travelers.
Location: Av. Scalabrini Ortiz 1331, Palermo, C1425DOA.
Hours: Daily, 7:00 p.m.–3:00 a.m.
Cost: ARS 8,000 (USD $10).

La Viruta
La Viruta is a lively, youthful milonga where beginners and experts mingle. Nights start with lessons, then transform into all-night dance sessions until 6:00 a.m. It's one of the best places for first-timers.
Location: Armenia 1366, Palermo, C1414DKD.
Hours: Thu–Sun, until 6:00 a.m.
Cost: ARS 7,500 (USD $9).

Club Gricel
Traditional and old-school, Club Gricel has been running for decades. Locals of all ages gather here, and the atmosphere is friendly but steeped in tradition. Perfect for travelers who want an authentic tango night.
Location: La Rioja 1180, San Cristóbal, C1244ADC.
Hours: Mon–Sat, evenings until late.
Cost: ARS 7,000 (USD $8).

Quiet Parks & Local Hangouts
Plaza Armenia

In the heart of Palermo Soho, Plaza Armenia is a leafy square surrounded by trendy cafés and design shops. It's perfect for people-watching between shopping sprees. On weekends, artisan stalls pop up selling crafts.
Location: Costa Rica & Armenia, Palermo.
Hours: 24/7.
Cost: Free.

Plaza Dorrego (on weekdays)
When the Sunday antique fair isn't on, Plaza Dorrego is a quiet, atmospheric square. Locals play chess, sip coffee at outdoor cafés, and occasionally impromptu tango dancers perform in the evenings.
Location: Defensa & Humberto 1°, San Telmo.
Hours: 24/7.
Cost: Free.

Parque Lezama
One of the city's most historic parks, said to be the site of Buenos Aires' first foundation. It features sculptures, tree-lined paths, and the

National Historical Museum at its edge. On weekends, families picnic and informal markets appear.
Location: Av. Brasil & Defensa, San Telmo.
Hours: Daily, 7:00 a.m.–9:00 p.m.
Cost: Free.

Plaza Francia (Recoleta)
Set next to Recoleta Cemetery, this shady plaza is home to a weekend artisan fair, while during the week it's a peaceful hangout for students and locals. Great spot for picnics under trees.
Location: Av. del Libertador & Av. Pueyrredón, Recoleta.
Hours: 24/7.
Cost: Free.

Reserva Ecológica Costanera Sur (quiet trails)
Beyond the main entrances, the ecological reserve has hidden lagoons and peaceful trails perfect for bird-watching. It's an unexpected slice of wilderness minutes from skyscrapers.
Location: Av. Tristán Achával Rodríguez 1550, Puerto Madero.
Hours: Tue–Sun, 8:00 a.m.–6:00 p.m.
Cost: Free.

CHAPTER 9: LANGUAGE, ETIQUETTE & COMMUNICATION

Essential Spanish Phrases for Travelers

While many younger Argentines in Buenos Aires speak some English, a little Spanish goes a long way. Argentines are warm and receptive when visitors make the effort. Locals speak Rioplatense Spanish, a variant with Italian-style intonation and unique vocabulary (like "vos" instead of "tú").

Useful Phrases:
- Hello – Hola
- Good morning – Buenos días
- Good afternoon – Buenas tardes
- Good evening/night – Buenas noches
- Please – Por favor
- Thank you – Gracias
- You're welcome – De nada
- Excuse me / Sorry – Perdón / Disculpe
- Do you speak English? – ¿Habla inglés?
- How much does it cost? – ¿Cuánto cuesta?
- I'd like this one – Quiero este
- Where is…? – ¿Dónde está…?
- A coffee, please – Un café, por favor
- The bill, please – La cuenta, por favor
- Cheers! – ¡Salud!

Traveler Tip: Porteños (locals) often say "chau" instead of "adiós" for goodbye — a remnant of Italian influence.

Polite Customs & Social Etiquette

Greetings: In Argentina, even strangers often greet with a single kiss on the cheek (left cheek). A handshake may be used in formal business settings.

Personal Space: Argentines stand closer when conversing, and touching a friend's arm or shoulder is common. Don't pull back — it may be seen as cold.

Dining Etiquette: Dinner usually starts late (9:00 p.m. or later). It's polite to linger after meals; rushing away can feel rude.

Tipping: Around 10% in restaurants is expected unless included in the bill. Leave cash tips, as service charges on credit cards often don't go to staff.

Punctuality: Social gatherings run late. Arriving 15–30 minutes after the scheduled time is normal, even expected.

Conversation: Locals enjoy debating politics, football, and philosophy. Engaging passionately is welcomed, but avoid condescending tones.

Traveler Insight: If invited to someone's home, bring wine, pastries, or flowers. Avoid gifts in purple or black, which are associated with mourning.

How to Interact with Locals

Positive Interactions:
- Show enthusiasm for tango, football, and Argentine food — these are sources of pride.

- Use vos (informal "you") instead of "tú." Example: ¿Cómo estás vos? instead of ¿Cómo estás tú?

- Make eye contact; Argentines appreciate directness and warmth.

What to Avoid:
- Don't compare Argentina negatively with Brazil or Chile — it touches on regional rivalries.

- Avoid calling Buenos Aires "the Paris of South America" directly to locals. They prefer pride in Argentina's own identity.

- Don't complain about inflation or politics unless you're invited into the topic — locals are passionate, but sensitive.

- Never say "soccer" — it's fútbol. And avoid disrespecting Boca Juniors or River Plate unless you want heated banter.

Traveler Tip: Humor and expressive body language go far. Argentines often joke with strangers, especially in markets or taxis.

Using English vs. Spanish in 2026

In 2026, English will be widely taught in schools, and you'll find decent English spoken in hotels, airports, upscale restaurants, and major attractions. But outside these areas:

- **Public Transport:** Ticket sellers and bus drivers rarely speak English.

- **Markets & Fairs:** Most artisans don't speak English, but they're patient if you use gestures or basic Spanish.

- **Older Generations:** Many older Porteños may not understand English at all.

Traveler Strategy: Use Spanish greetings and basics, then switch to English if necessary. Many locals will try to help with what English they know, and some will happily practice their skills.

SIM Cards, Internet & Staying Connected

Buenos Aires is one of South America's most connected cities, with strong 4G coverage and expanding 5G services in central neighborhoods by 2026.

SIM Cards
Three main providers dominate:
1. Claro Argentina – Wide coverage, especially in Buenos Aires and major highways.

2. Movistar – Strongest in cities, competitive prepaid data packages.

3. Personal – Often cheapest prepaid options, good in Buenos Aires but weaker in rural areas.

Cost: SIM cards cost around ARS 2,000 (USD $2.50). A 10 GB prepaid package for 7 days is about ARS 10,000 (USD $12).

Where to Buy: Airport kiosks (EZE and AEP), convenience stores, official brand stores, or large supermarkets. Passport is required for registration.

Wi-Fi Access
Cafés, hotels, and even parks in Buenos Aires offer free Wi-Fi. Palermo, Recoleta, and Microcentro plazas have city-provided hotspots.

Speeds average 20–50 Mbps, enough for video calls.

eSIMs

For travelers with compatible phones, eSIM services like Airalo and Holafly are increasingly popular. Prices are slightly higher but convenient if you don't want to change physical SIMs.

Traveler Insight: Download Google Translate offline Spanish and ride-hailing apps like Cabify before arrival. Local taxis don't always accept credit cards, so apps can bridge language and payment gaps.

CHAPTER 10: PRACTICAL TIPS FOR TRAVELERS

Currency & Money Matters

In 2026, Argentina continues to experience economic volatility, meaning travelers should be savvy about handling money. The official currency is the Argentine Peso (ARS), and while inflation remains high, digital payments and multiple exchange rates are common.

Exchange Rates: In 2026, the official rate and informal "dólar blue" (street rate) still exist. Many travelers exchange USD or EUR at official exchange houses (casas de cambio), but also through informal channels that often offer better value. Always use reputable sources — never street hawkers.

ATMs: Available but expensive. Withdrawal fees can be ARS 4,000–5,000 (USD $5–6) per transaction with low withdrawal limits.

Cards: Credit and debit cards are widely accepted in restaurants, malls, and hotels, but some small shops, markets, and taxis only accept cash. Visa and Mastercard are the most reliable.

Digital Wallets: Apps like Mercado Pago are commonly used by locals. Some cafés and stores accept QR code payments, but these usually require a local account.

Traveler Strategy: Bring USD or EUR in cash and exchange gradually. Avoid exchanging large amounts at once, since the peso loses value quickly.

Traveler Insight: Always carry some small bills and coins for buses, tips, or small cafés. Some vendors won't accept torn or damaged notes.

Safety & Common Scams

Buenos Aires is generally safe for travelers, but like many big cities, it has its share of petty crime.

Pickpocketing: Common in crowded areas such as San Telmo Market, Subte trains, and Florida Street. Use crossbody bags and keep valuables close.

"Mustard Scam": Someone spills liquid on you (mustard, ketchup, etc.) and offers to "help clean it," while an accomplice steals your wallet. Politely decline and walk away.

Taxi Scams: Some drivers claim their meter is broken or give fake change. Use official taxis (radio taxis) or ridesharing apps like Cabify or Uber for security.

ATM Scams: Avoid standalone ATMs on the street. Use machines inside banks or malls.

Counterfeit Bills: Be cautious with ARS 1,000+ notes. Feel for watermarks and texture.

Traveler Insight: Violent crime is rare in tourist areas, but avoid flashing expensive jewelry or cameras at night. Stick to well-lit, busy streets in San Telmo, La Boca, and Microcentro after dark.

Emergency Numbers:
- Police: 911
- Tourist Police (multilingual assistance): +54 11 4346-5748
- Ambulance: 107
- Fire Department: 100

Health, Emergency Numbers & Pharmacies

Water Safety: Tap water is technically safe but may upset sensitive stomachs. Bottled water is cheap (ARS 1,500 / USD $2 per liter).

Food Safety: Street food is generally safe, especially in San Telmo and Palermo, but always check for freshness.

Pharmacies: Known as farmacias, they are common in every neighborhood. Most carry both prescription and over-the-counter medication. Chain pharmacies like Farmacity often stay open late.

Hospitals: Public hospitals provide free emergency care, even for foreigners, though wait times can be long. Private hospitals like Hospital Alemán and Hospital Italiano offer faster, higher-quality care but may require upfront payment.

Traveler Insight: Bring sunscreen and mosquito repellent in summer months (December–February). Pharmacies also sell prepaid SIMs, making them handy one-stop shops.

Packing List Essentials for Buenos Aires

Clothing:
- Summer (Dec–Feb): Light, breathable clothes, sunhat, sunglasses.
- Winter (Jun–Aug): Jacket, layers, scarf (temperatures can drop to 8°C / 46°F at night).
- Year-round: Comfortable walking shoes — Buenos Aires' cobblestones can be tricky.

Extras:
- Reusable water bottle (eco-friendly & practical).
- Power adapter: Argentina uses Type C and Type I plugs, 220V supply.

- Small backpack or crossbody bag for day trips and to deter pickpockets.
- Spanish phrasebook or offline translation app.
- Portable umbrella — sudden rain showers are common.

Traveler Insight: Porteños dress stylishly, even casually. Blending in with smart-casual attire (jeans, shirts, dresses) will help you feel less like a tourist.

Seasonal Weather Guide

Buenos Aires has four distinct seasons, though its temperate climate makes it a year-round destination.

Summer (Dec–Feb): Hot and humid, with temperatures often above 30°C (86°F). Great for nightlife and outdoor dining, but sightseeing can be tiring. Expect afternoon thunderstorms.

Autumn (Mar–May): Mild and comfortable (15–25°C / 59–77°F). A beautiful time for strolling parks and enjoying outdoor cafés. Prices are lower outside Easter.

Winter (Jun–Aug): Cool but not harsh (8–15°C / 46–59°F). Ideal for museums, tango shows, and café culture. Rarely drops below 5°C (41°F).

Spring (Sep–Nov): Perhaps the best season. Jacaranda trees bloom in purple across Recoleta and Palermo, temperatures hover around 20–25°C (68–77°F), and festivals fill the city.

Best Time to Visit: Spring (Sep–Nov) and Autumn (Mar–May) strike the best balance of pleasant weather, fewer crowds, and affordable prices.

CONCLUSION

Why Buenos Aires Will Leave You Wanting More

Buenos Aires is a city that lingers with you long after you've left. It's not just about the grand avenues, tango shows, and sizzling steaks—it's about the rhythm of daily life and the energy of its people. The city moves at its own pace: mornings filled with strong coffee and medialunas, afternoons of wandering leafy plazas or debating football at the corner café, and nights that stretch until dawn with music, dance, and conversation.

Each neighborhood reveals a different character. San Telmo's cobblestones whisper of colonial days, La Boca bursts with color and passion, Recoleta radiates elegance, while Palermo reinvents itself constantly with design, food, and nightlife. Buenos Aires isn't just a place to see — it's a place to feel, to taste, to hear, and to live.

Inspiring Final Thoughts

By the end of your journey, you'll find yourself captivated not only by the landmarks but by the moments in between: the spontaneous street tango that stops you mid-walk, the generous pour of Malbec in a tucked-away wine bar, or the warmth of a porteño who insists you share in their mate ritual.

Buenos Aires is a city of contrasts—old yet modern, chaotic yet graceful, deeply Argentine yet globally connected. That balance gives it a magnetic pull, drawing travelers back again and again.

So whether you came for three days or three weeks, expect to leave with more than photos. You'll take home stories, flavors, and melodies that call you back. Buenos Aires doesn't just show itself—it becomes part of you.

And that is why, for most who visit, one trip is never enough.

Printed in Dunstable, United Kingdom